I0101194

Republican Hypocrisy: 33 Reasons Why Republicans Are Hypocrites

By Mike Aiken

Contents

Introduction

Since the...questionable results of the 2000 election, many have had serious questions and doubts regarding the Republican Party. These stem from many things, such as sketchy policy or general incompetence, but they all come down to one word: hypocrisy. Hypocrisy in the sense of saying one thing but doing another, in the sense of lying to the public, and even in the sense of doing the exact thing they are criticizing. This hypocrisy permeates through all different parts of the Republican Party, and surrounds many different policies, statements agendas. Many higher ups in the Republican Party will routinely say one thing, and then, based on circumstance or convenience, will do something completely different.

All different types and examples of these hypocrisies will be explored in detail throughout the following pages. In order to do this, we will look at various incidents that will help us understand why and how the Republican Party operates in the way that they do. Deceit is not the same thing as hypocrisy, but one usually follows the other, especially in politics. Each of these gives a piece of the overall hypocrisy, and in this guide you will see why you can't believe everything you hear.

Sometimes, political policy is shrouded in mystery or works in a confusing way. However, sometimes, as is the case with the sections that will follow, it just doesn't make any sense. Stating your beliefs is a fine, normal way to approach the political sphere. In fact, today's bipartisan system depends on the differing of beliefs to function in the way that it does. However, using those beliefs as a way to skew your own agenda, or to further your own needs, is not a good way to keep a healthy, open policy. The Republican agenda has long been a shifting one; something that constantly changes based on a certain policy or time of the year. Yes, Republicans tend to get a bad rap in this country, but, as you will soon see, this bad rap is largely earned. Each section will cover a certain area of politics, a topic that has contributed the way things are currently run in Washington, and then we will explore how Republicans have decided to approach said topics.

Hypocrisy is not something that has to be entwined with politics. Sometimes it is ok to be honest, to stick with your values and keep your moral conduct. Unfortunately, the Republican Party has to intention to follow that dogma. Rather, they follow votes, money and power, all of which they will do whatever it takes to get. This guide will serve two purposes in this way. One, it will hope to better shed light on or expose the way the Republican Party has chosen to operate over the past few years. Two, it will point out some inherent wrongs that exists within their political agenda, and, while many of those wrong can be attributed to different things, they all come together under one word: hypocrisy.

1. Not Following the Bible

While the list of Republican hypocrisy is both long and extensive, we will begin by looking at one of the biggest tropes associated with the party: religion. More specifically, Christian or Catholic tropes and values. Now, there is nothing wrong with being religious or having faith, but many members of the Republican Party often take quotes from the Bible and then use them out of context. In this way, while it sounds like the quotes they are using backup their points, a little research (as it most often does) destroys the validity of these arguments. Practicing religion or following your own beliefs is a fine way to live your life. However, taking those quotes out of context for the purposes of a questionable political agenda is most certainly not.

We will begin this section by studying a Republican Representative in North Dakota by the name of Kevin Kramer. Kramer, in all of his political wisdom, felt like it was a good idea to cut food stamps. For those that are not aware, food stamps are very important to many low-income workers and families who do not make enough to support themselves or their children. They can give workers extra help, and even take some pressure off of their daily lives. Unfortunately, none of that really mattered to Kramer. As a result, he started to build an agenda to cut the food stamp plan entirely. When justifying his actions, what text did he quote? You guessed it, the good old Bible.

When answering questions about this policy, Kramer quoted the Bible, stating "If anyone is not willing to work, let him not eat". This quote, on the surface, supports exactly what Kramer is preaching. Yet, it also raises another very interesting point. Taking a passage from the Bible in order to meet a certain agenda is a direct refutation of what Jesus taught. Many of Jesus' teachings were about helping others and bringing equality to those who did not have the same opportunities as you. Not only is Kramer trying to do the opposite of that through his food stamp policy, but he also is disparaging the Bible while doing so as well. In this case, the quote may not be exactly misconstrued, but the motives and methods behind using it most certainly are.

Mr. Kramer has no problem ignoring the Bible's teachings, and another popular Republican, Mitt Romney, is the exact same way. However, Romney's hypocrisy stems from a very rampant debate right now; climate change. The planet needs us, regardless of what many certain political leaders may think. Of course, if you're not a fan of science, or if you're not a fan of actually following the Bible's teachings, you can be like Romney. When running in 2012, Romney said he was not running for President in order to slow the rise of the oceans or to help the planet heal. This goes directly against one of Christ's most basic teachings, which is to help others and care for our fellow man. The planet, while divided by boundaries both political and geographical, is one whole organism. By refusing to help take care of it, you are also refusing to help out other human beings.

In a similar vein, Romney has also said he was not concerned for the very poor due to the fact that we have a safety net in place to help them. Not only is this a convenient line of thinking for someone who has millions of dollars to their name, but it once again goes against the Bible's most basic teachings. Not helping the poor is directly refuting the phrase "help your fellow man". It is very easy to claim to adopt a value or teaching, but to actually live following those rules is another story entirely.

Bill O'Reilly, another fun-loving Republican who happens to be the face of a very successful talk show, has led a crusade against Christmas for some time. This crusade was called the "War on Christmas" and appeared on Fox News. In this fight, O'Reilly has insisted that we keep the "Christ" in Christmas as a way to stick to our Christian roots. However, like the two people above, he says one thing while actively doing another. In this case, it is criticizing the poor. O'Reilly has repeatedly demonized those that are poor by claiming that they are solely responsible for the position that they are in. Ignoring the obvious flaws with that argument, which attributes nothing to factors such as opportunity or environment; this is another statement that ignores the whole "help your fellow man" thing the Bible is so insistent on.

Jesus' values revolve around giving to those in need, not criticizing them. All three of these men, while claiming they follow and believe in the Bible's teachings, do not actually live by this code. For a party who prides themselves on following the values of Christ, they sure seem to be missing a thing or two. This is a glaring example of hypocrisy within their party, and just one that will be covered in these pages.

2. Unemployment

This next section, while moving away from topics of religion, will stay focused on creating a disparity between the rich and the poor. This is a theme that will be seen many times in this guide, which is mainly due to the fact that Republicans tend to put favor towards the rich as opposed the poor. A lot of the people in this guide have quite a lot of money and, if politics have taught us anything, people with a lot of money tend to try to use their resources to help other people who have a lot of money.

Take for instance, the Republican duo of John Boehner and Mitch McConnell. Boehner is a speaker at the House of Representative and McConnell is a senator from Kentucky. However, they both have very similar mindsets, and each agrees with the other's thinking. This is why they stated that we need to eliminate unemployment benefits in America. Not a bad idea, for those who are not unemployed. However, for those who are, these benefits can be very key in keeping them alive and helping them get back on their feet during tough times.

That being said, these men do have a point when they have said that unemployment benefits were only supposed to be a temporary fix. However, they are still in place years after their inception, which is not what they were intended for. A valid point, except when that same logic is applied to wealthy tax cuts. Both men have stated that it is necessary to keep tax cuts for the wealthy. Why? Because those cuts have already been in place for ten years, and as such, there is no reason to stop them now. Except for the fact that, that is the same logic they use for cutting down unemployment benefits. It is not simply that cutting unemployment benefits may hurt some people who rely on them to live, but more so that they these men put their own needs before others and hide it behind a curtain. The line of "we've been doing for a long time, so why stop" does not hold up under this type of thinking, and points out the way their hypocrisy works. This can be further reviewed in this interview with John Stewart (http://www.politicususa.com/2014/01/10/jon-stewart-hammers-conservatives-hypocrisy-income-inequality.html).

The next example, while not necessarily a lesson in hypocrisy, does show what happens when people tend to formulate and follow their own plans. This is the case of Sam Brownback, the Republican Governor of Kansas. During his term, Brownback came up with a genius plan to run his own social experiment. On that should not only have not been pursued, but on that was a bold move which yielded very little payoff...though we'll get to that in a minute.

The experiment in question was when Brownback decided to implement a hefty tax cut for the rich that also, as an added bonus, deprived schools of necessary funding they would need for things like books or after school programs. You know, useless stuff like that. This move was made as an attempt for the Governor to restore the lost funding that schools had lost during the recession. However, it, as predicted, did not work out exactly as Brownback had planned. Now, years later, this experiment has been considered a huge failure. This is mainly due to the fact that the program did not produce anything close to the results that Brownback was hoping to see. In fact, it has actually increased poverty levels across the state and led to a whopping $300 million revenue shortfall. That's a lot more problematic than losing funding to schools, which hurts the entire state. Of course, except for the ones who got the tax cuts, they're doing just fine.

Now, in his run for re-election, Brownback is promising to spend more time and focus more of his energy on helping the poor. However, it seems that this may come a little too late. The people who really got hurt from the deficit caused by these tax cuts have reported that they believe the path that Brownback took should not have been pursued at all. This is a perfect example of saying one thing just to meet your current needs. It is very easy to say that you value the poor and want to focus on curbing poverty after you have already made a move that crippled them. However, it is not just the poor who have suffered, but the entire state. John Boehner and Mitch McConnell may be using flawed logic in their arguments against unemployment benefits, but at least when they are hurting the poor they own up to it. Here, it is just shrouded behind a man attempting to run for another term after he already botched the first.

3. No One Can Die When Obama's President

When discussing the motives and movements of the Republican Party, it is almost impossible to ignore the subject of Barack Obama. His policy has long been under fire by members of the party, as has his foreign policy and military ideology. Here, we will look at that ideology and analyze exactly why and how Republicans attack it. More importantly, we will understand why their thinking and reasons are deeply flawed. It is not necessarily that Obama's motives are right, but rather that the reasons behind attacking these motives are most definitely wrong.

The main event that we will cite in this section is the attacks in the U.S. Embassy in Benghazi on September 11, 2012. During these attacks, four Americans were killed, a tragedy that led to a natural backlash against the Obama campaign. Many Republicans used this incident to fuel fires, stating the attacks and their aftermath were mishandled throughout the entire process. Ted Cruz, who will learn more about later, even went as far to accuse Hillary Clinton of purposely blocking information to the public in order to make the mishandling seem better than it actually was. Not only was this thinking flawed, but it also revealed a large amount of hypocrisy that occurred during the time before Obama.

While Bush was in office, there were a number of attacks on U.S. Embassy and its consulates. During all of these, to reveal the obvious hypocrisy of these practices, there was very little rage over these attacks compared to the attacks at Benghazi. In total, during the eight years that Bush was in office, there were sixty total deaths at these different embassies. These attacks yielded almost no outcry from the heads of the Republican Party. However, when four people are attacked under Obama's term, Republicans make it seem like it was the worst thing that has ever happened. Here is a list all of the attacks that went unnoticed during Bush's term: five killed at U.S. Embassy at Kolkata, twelve killed at U.S. Embassy at Karachi, two killed at the U.S. Embassy at Islamabad, two killed at the U.S. Embassy at Tashkent, nine killed at the US compound in Saudi Arabia, two killed at the U.S. Embassy in Karachi, four killed at the U.S. Embassy at Syria, two killed at the U.S. Embassy in Yemen, six killed at the U.S. Embassy in Istanbul, and at the U.S. Embassy at Yemen, sixteen people were killed.

The most widely known of all instances is, of course, September 11th, 2001, when the World Trade Center towers fell. This incident led to an invasion of Afghanistan. However, our soldiers were not currently in Afghanistan, they were in Iraq -- strange how that works. The invasion of Iraq, which has costs thousands upon thousands American lives, had very little opposition or outcry when it happened. That point took what was supposed to be a quick war for Osama Bin Laden, and turned it into a multi-year affair that is still going on today. However, the lives lost due to the war have not been acknowledged or spoken about by Republicans currently in office today. This is the basis of hypocrisy, and a perfect example of picking and choosing when to care about things and when to not.

All of the attacks on the U.S. Embassy and its consulates were spread out, but cost many lives that went relatively unnoticed. When the attack on the U.S. Consulate in Karachi and Pakistan were attacked in 2002, ten Americans were killed. Silence followed the attacks from the Republican Party, which was even worse as they had the presidency at the time. In 2008, another ten Americans were killed during a bombing at the U.S. Embassy in Yemen. Silence followed from the Republican Party once again.

12

In this light, it seems very strange (hypocritical some would say) that Republicans have spent so much time outraging about Obama's incompetence when it comes to handling what happened at Benghazi, but ignored so many similar incidents that happened during the Bush administration. It is one thing to get upset over the loss of human lives, that is natural response to such things, but when you ignore sixty lost lives for the sake of your own administration, that is a different story altogether. They even went as far as to call many of the deaths that happened under Bush "unfortunate accidents". However, when the same things happened under Obama, they were a tragedy. The loss of many American live is a tragedy no matter how you swing it. And the lives matter, no matter if they are lost during a time where Obama is in office, or if they were lost under Bush. Choosing to look the other way for some and not for others is a gross reaction to something that have should more meaning.

4. Republicans Support Women's Rights... to Vote for Them

For this next section, we will be taking a trip back into history. Specifically, a trip back to a time long before we had anything as simple as civil or equal rights. Let's go back to 1920, a time of prohibition and long dresses, of factories and early cars. This was the year when women first got the right to vote; a seemingly simple issue, but one that is becoming one of the foremost issues that the Republican Party is currently facing. Why? Because the female vote is something the party is currently lacking. Republicans want to get women to vote for them; however, in line with the above problems we have already covered, they are not making any strides towards helping women or garnering their vote.

The first, and most important, question that needs to be answered is why would any woman vote for the Republican Party? In order to understand this, we need to properly analyze the way party members have treated women, as well as the statements they have made describing the fairer gender. Sometimes, it seems as if the entire political party has forgotten about women completely. While it is nice to say one thing (as in the case of the Benghazi incident) following through on the thing you say is a whole different story. Actions, as they always have, speak so much louder than words, and here we will cover some of the more extreme ways that Republicans have spoken out against the female gender. These actions have given Democrats all the more reason to continue asserting their message that the GOP is waging a "war on women".

There are plenty of hypocritical actions the party has taken against women, but we will start with the example of Mike

Huckabee. Huckabee served at the 44th governor of Kansas, and during that time has made multiple statements regarding birth control. He believes that the government should not be responsible for providing birth control to women; a strange belief, and one that really shows his true feelings about such serious issues. How, you might be wondering, exactly does he hope to fix this problem? Huckabee tells women to control themselves and not have so much sex with men. This type of blaming not only proposes a completely unrealistic solution to the world, but it also proposes a completely unrealistic way of thinking.

Don't believe it's true? Listen to this quote from Huckabee: "If the Democrats want to insult the women of America by making them believe that they are helpless without Uncle Sugar coming in and providing for them a prescription each month for birth control because they cannot control their libido or their reproductive system without the help of the government, then so be it. Let us take that discussion all across America, because women are far more than the Democrats have played them to be". Real nice. During his attempts to disagree with the way that birth control is often used, and in his attempt to make it look like the Democrats don't care about women, Huckabee inadvertently showed his true colors.

Next we have Todd Akin, an ex-congressman and Republican Senate nominee in Missouri, found himself in a very awkward position in 2012. This was when he tried to explain his stance on abortion and instances of "legitimate rape". That's right, legitimate rape. What exactly does that mean? "If it's a legitimate rape," Aki said, "The female body has ways to try to shut that whole thing down. But let's assume that maybe that didn't work or something: I think there should be some punishment, but the punishment ought to be of the rapist, and not attacking the child." This shows a lot of focus on his personal ideas about abortion, but shows little compassion for women.

Rush Limbaugh, one of the voices of the party, was quoted saying that college co-ed Susan Fluke was a slut for asking the government to pay for her birth control. Yes, calling her a slut for simply asking for a right that should be afforded to all women. In 2011, Rep. Chris Smith of New Jersey also made his move against women by introducing the "No Taxpayer Funding for Abortion Act". This act is in place to permanently stop federal funding for abortions. Richard Mourdock also stunned many when he said a pregnancy resulting from rape is God's intention.

Statements such as these are contributing to a gender gap between the Republicans and the Democrats that does not favor the Republicans at all. This is a problem for the party, and is very hypocritical because they still have the nerve to ask for women voters before spurning them with their actions. This makes no sense on two different levels. On one hand, it is very bad public policy, isolating half of the country with ignorant statements. On the other, it reeks of hypocrisy. You cannot say you want women's votes but then treat them or ignore them in this manner. It just doesn't work in that way.

5. Republicans Only Support Veterans When They Fight

Another big problem for Republicans is the subject of veterans. Veterans and veteran care have been really big issues as of late and, like any big issue, they are a really good example of the incompetence and hypocrisy that the Republican Party exudes. On the surface, it seems like a really complicated solution with a generally simple fix. You let veterans have access to benefits, and give them support for the service they did for our country. While that is simple, the Republican Party doesn't really see it that way. In fact, they act in almost the exact opposite way.

The very nature of hypocrisy stems from flip-flopping, or saying one thing on an issue while doing something else. In this case, that revolves around veterans supporting both war and our soldiers, but no longer supporting those same soldiers once they are done fighting.

This was outlined in 2012 when Republicans shot down a bill that would give aid to and help veterans once they had returned to back home. It seems that many of the party deemed that it would be too costly to help these men and women, even going as far as to say that the bill might undermine the economy of the nation. However, supporting someone when they are doing what you want (fighting a war) and then pulling the rug out from under them after they have done their duty isn't just hypocritical, it's also wrong. U.S Senate Republicans also blocked legislation that would have expanded federal healthcare and education programs for veterans, saying the $24 billion bill would bust the budget. Wouldn't it make sense that a person, who is willing to die for our opportunities to be safe and live in a free country, would still be that same person once their time in the war was over? And wouldn't it make sense that, if you are so driven to get those people to fight for you, you would help them after they have helped you? Of course it does. Well, maybe not if you are a member of the Republican Party, and especially not if you are Tom Coburn.

Tom Coburn was the junior states senator of Oklahoma, and during the time he was in office, he made some comments regarding veterans who were coming back from the Iraq War, a war that was started and pushed by the Republicans when Bush was in office. In this statement, Coburn said that helping pass this bill, in accordance with others, would undermine the nation's economy. While the price tag on the bill (somewhere around $24 billion) was high, there is no reason to pull support on these grounds, especially for those who were so adamant about the war the soldiers are fighting in.

Very similar to the above section, this is an example of Republicans giving great support for one thing, but only for the time that it furthers their needs. Supporting our troops means supporting them throughout their entire lives, not just during the time when they can serve or give service to the war. Even after the war is over, they still deserve those same rights. It is not easy to be a soldier returning home, and, due to their service, the people who headed the war should be eager to support them in their endeavor. Unfortunately, this is not the case, and so many veterans, due to the hypocrisy of the Republican Party, have been left without a proper way to integrate back into normal society.

The bill in question would have had additional benefits for veterans as well, such as a measure that would have brought the most significant changes in decades to the U.S. veterans' programs.

For example, it called for twenty-seven new medical facilities to help a healthcare system that is strained by veterans of the Iraq and Afghanistan wars. It is clear that Republicans show a great amount of respect to the soldiers who fight in their wars, even in the event of a wars we shouldn't have been in (like Iraq), but once those soldiers need a little bit of help to get back on their feet, those same Republicans are nowhere to be found.

For the past six years, Republicans have adopted extreme measures, and give outrageous arguments to oppose President Obama and congressional Democrat's myriad initiatives and legislation to help Veterans find any kind of work, access job training, or get the benefits that anyone who "supports the troops" should provide. This blocking was so extreme that Obama actually took matters into his own hands and announced that 50,000 Veterans would receive training in the growing solar panel industry. Though that move should have been backed by Republicans, as it helped those they readily call "American's Heroes" it was not backed by them at all, as those "heroes" were no longer fighting their war.

6. Pro-Life, but Just for Fetuses

Next, we will look at one of the touchiest subjects that will be covered in this guide, as well as one of the touchiest subjects covered in modern politics: abortion. It seems like this would be pretty clean cut, as most members of the Republican Party are open about how they feel about abortion. However, this section goes beyond just abortion. Many Republicans take the stance of being "Pro-life". This means that they are inherently against the act of abortion and believe that all fetuses are living human beings. This section will not debate that fact, but rather look at the term "Pro-life" and discuss how the Republican Party is anything but.

It's one thing to use a term that sounds good, such as "Pro-life" in your speeches, but if your policy, statements, and leaders don't actually show regard for human life, does it matter? That's a very important question, and one that deserves a closer look. The main problem with "Pro-life" policy is that it seems Republicans only use that phrase when it's centered around abortions. In fact, due to many actions that we will see, one could easily argue that Republicans are all for a "Pro-life" stance, but only when the life in question is a fetus. They stop caring about that life once the fetus is born. That's a lot like thinking that, say, soldiers are ok to support as long as they are in the war, but no longer need to be supported after.

As always, we will analyze this topic further by looking at a specific member of the Republican Party. That person here is Texas Governor Rick Perry. While his stance on the sanctity of life when it comes to abortion is very loud and clear, it gets a little more fuzzy when it comes to a life that isn't a fetus. During an interview, Perry publicly bragged about the number of executions that happen in his

23

state. This seems a bit hypocritical when it comes to someone who claims to be "Pro-life". Of course, the people who are being executed are criminals, but that does not mean they aren't worth as much as someone else. Furthermore, taking pride in the number of lives you take does not reflect that you truly believe in the sanctity of life.

Moving along on how Republicans care little about anyone who leaves the womb, there is also the matter of guns and war. War is a heavy toll that has taken the lives of thousands of Americans. The war in Iraq was almost exclusively pushed through by the Republican Party in a reach for resources and oil. The lives that were lost in that war matter too, and yet the Republicans who sent those soldiers to war seemed to have very little care for those lives. In addition, "Pro-life" seems to be stretched a little thin when it comes from people who are so gung-ho about making guns readily available. Republicans today want to have guns as means of protection, but also as showmanship. This means that they would be able to take firearms into a variety of public places such as family restaurants, bars, classrooms and churches. On average, statistics show that three people are killed by a gun every hour and approximately seven are shot. This shows the danger of guns, and their tendency to take human lives. As such, why would a group who claims to be "Pro-life" be so supportive of something that takes so many lives so readily available? These are the type of question that poke holes in the Republicans already thin beliefs.

One of the last aspects of "Pro-life", which has already been touched upon, is taking care of a child once they exit the womb. It makes very little sense to push policy in order to make sure women have to have their children, but then do nothing and offer no support for those children once they are born. Republicans have many policies that are built around not giving these mothers, whose children Republicans say they must have, support once they need to raise a child. The Republican Party routinely fights food stamp programs, which offer great support to women who have to raise a newborn child. Republicans also work hard to fight pushes for a livable minimum wage, another element that aids in raising a child. Not only does this once again go against the idea of policy that is truly "Pro-life", but it is also serves as another bill that would greatly help mothers who are trying to support a child. The basic necessities afforded by the increase in livable wages would be a huge boon for these mothers, but interestingly, as much as they are there when women are pregnant, Republicans are quite absent once the baby is out of the womb. If Republicans are going to vote for a mother to keep her child, they better be willing to help her raise it.

7. Republicans Want Hispanic Votes, Just Not Their Presence

This section will cover a topic that in many ways shows the same holes in the Republican agenda that the topic of women does. In the case of female voters, Republicans have said time and time again they desire the women vote, but have also said many things against that gender. This is a very bad policy, and is another example of a hypocritical agenda. This same hypocrisy is seen when the Republican Party tries to appeal to the Hispanic community.

Immigration is a very large, very heated political topic, and rightfully so. Hispanics are becoming one of the largest groups in today's America. Furthermore, they are also concentrated in some of the most important states for voting. California, Texas and Florida have so many large Latino populations that it makes perfect sense the Latino vote can easily help decided votes in such states. And, these three states are some of the biggest in the nation. Florida also is one of the most popular swing states. In Florida, Latino voters are predicted to top 1.6 million in 2012, a 34 percent increase in four years. As such, they also mean a lot of votes, which is particularly important to both political parties. It makes sense that Republicans would do what they can to get Latino communities on their side. Just as with women, Republicans have been saying that they support Hispanics and Hispanic populations as a way to try and sway those votes to their side. However, just as with women, they are also practicing something that is quite different from what they preach.

It is not simply that Latinos do not want to vote for the Republican Party, but that they have plenty of reasons to not vote for the Republican Party. There are multiple examples of this, which we will cover in this section, but the first is the fact that Republicans have routinely shot down legislation that would help grant U.S. citizenship, one of the biggest battles the Latino community is facing. This makes no sense for two reasons: one, if Republicans were set on getting Latino votes, they would help them as much as possible to foster this support, and two, if those Latinos the Republicans claim they are so set on helping are not citizens, then they cannot vote. This type of vicious circle is one of the main reasons the Latino population has no reason to vote with the party.

Immigration is at the heart of this issue, but many Republicans and heads of the Republican Party shy away from such talk whenever possible. They would rather sweep such issues under the rug than face them head on, which brings about no change or action. An example of this comes from Tim Pawlenty, a Republican who served as the 39th governor of Minnesota. He has stated that it would be a great disservice to only talk about immigration, because Hispanics care about other national issues as well. This is very true. However, while this sounds nice, it is merely a roundabout way of dodging the issue. By shrugging off such comments, politicians are able to negate the issue at hand. Do Latinos care about other issues? Of course they do. However, immigration should be discussed as well. Who are they to ask for Latino votes when they do nothing to aid one of the most important issues surrounding that population?

In addition to skirting around the issues of immigration, Republican Senator Lindsay Graham took the stance on the Latino population one step too far. Instead of merely suggesting ways to scale back on immigration (already not off to a great start) he decided to propose an idea to reject U.S citizenship to U.S born children. This may seem like a ridiculous solution, and that's because it is. So, you might wonder, how would this act even happen?

According to the Senator, it would happen by changing the Fourteenth Amendment of the Constitution to the United States of America. A simple fix, really, if you don't mind altering the way the country is run.

Graham's hypocrisy, which is a great microcosm of the hypocrisy of the party in general, goes even beyond his ludicrous idea to change the amendment. In the past, Graham has supported immigration reform, but has changed his mind along the way. He and his party are responsible for blocking reform in 2010. This was done by first holding the reform hostage to health care reform, pitting it against climate change legislation, and then turning his back on it altogether.

As the Hispanic community continues to grow in this nation, they also begin to hold more power. Currently, there are 50 million Latinos in the United States, and they have over 21 million voters. As stated, because those voters are in key states, they could be a central part to choosing the next president. The Hispanic community has grown to be so large in the United States that they now have the power to fight back. Lying and saying things you don't mean is not the way to get them onto your side. Take note, Republicans.

8. Vacation for Us and Nobody Else

Now, we will take a quick break from the heated debates that permeate throughout the politics of this country and examine a topic everyone can agree on: vacation. Vacation is a great, well-earned time that allows anyone, no matter what field of work they do or where they live, to experience some of the finer things in life. This also allows for some much needed rest, and gives a chance to spend time with family and loved ones. Simple enough, everyone can agree on that. But now it seems that Republican Party might have a thing or two to say about vacations as well.

Vacations, while mostly universal, can be a bit trickier when it comes to being the President of the United States. This is because, as you may know, the president cannot simply walk away from their duties or take a spontaneous trip to the Bahamas. There many moving parts when it comes to being President and you have to balance your work appropriately. Yes, the President does get vacations (more on that in a minute), but anything can interrupt that time should something important or dire occur. Even one simple phone call can sidetrack a vacation and make it so the President is back at the White House. This means that it is much more important for the President to take time off when he can. Even so, Republicans have not felt that this should be applied to Barack Obama.

When it comes to criticizing the President, it is very easy to key in on the time they are not in office. However, everyone, even the President, needs some down time every now and then. Republicans have expressed their displeasure of Obama taking some of this down time, and have deemed that Obama is taking too many vacation days.

31

On the surface, this seems like it could be a logical argument, but, as always, it pays to dig a little deeper. Here, we will go back and look at the last Republican President to better understand how hypocritical the Republican Party is being when they criticize Obama for taking some much needed time off.

George W. Bush, who served two terms as a Republican President of the United States, a man who pushed the Republican agenda, started a war and fought for oil, took more vacation days than any other President in the history of the United States. That's right, more than any other president in history. So far into his Presidency, Obama has embarked on nine "vacations". This brings his total amount of time off to forty-eight days. A good chunk of time and some of those trips did last around a week. However, George W. Bush, at the same point during his term, had visited his ranch in Crawford, Texas, a staggering fourteen times. And how many days did he spend there? One-hundred and fifteen days. That's a lot of vacation time. However, as quick as the Republicans are to criticize the amount of time Obama has spent with his family on vacation, they were silent during Bush's two terms. A little strange given that Bush's vacation time was more than double President Obama's. Even Ronald Reagan took more time away from the White House than Obama. Very interesting numbers, and another prime example of Republicans getting mad or upset only at people they don't support.

At one point during Obama's second run, Mitt Romney even took some shots at the president's vacation time. He claimed that, because Obama was taking such time off, he was an elitist. During this time, Obama was taking some trips to Martha's Vineyard. However, Romney himself often stays in a nearby neighborhood in his home state. This is another snapshot of criticizing something, while doing that exact thing yourself. If someone doesn't spend their time vacationing near Obama, then they might have something to say about the situation. However, calling him out for the very thing you do is not professional, and, as with so many different parts examined in these pages, makes very little sense.

9. No One Can Touch Our Guns

Now that the riveting topic of Obama's vacation and family time have been picked apart, we return in this section to look at a more serious topic. That topic is gun control, perhaps one of the most lively and controversial subjects in modern-day politics. It is no secret that Republicans tend to love their guns. And this does not just go for themselves, but they are also very adamant about guns being more available for people all across the United States; "Pro-gun" if you will. They do this by explaining or citing the Second Amendment of the Constitution. This amendment is the right to bear arms, which, as the name suggests, gives citizens the right to own and use their own, personal firearms. However, you don't have to go far to start noticing a pattern of hypocrisy in this line of thinking.

There have been many proposals to changing the gun laws in this country. This ranges through many different modes of reform, but they all center on restricting gun access, or attempting to make the world safer by making guns harder to come by. However, anytime such a measure is proposed, the Republican Party steps up and says that restricting guns is a direct violation of the Constitution. This may very well be true, but it is very convenient that the party uses the Constitution when it comes to protecting their guns, but they choose to ignore it for other factors that don't suit their needs.

Wiretapping, collecting private data, looking at phone records and other such acts are all illegal under the Constitution. However, there are many Republicans who actively support such measures under the largely false pretense of "national security". This is a very large hole in the gun argument, because you can't have the Constitution work both ways. It is not a document that works out of convenience, but rather out of law. In the mid-2000s, NASA got busted for collecting information on phone calls of the American people. This was a direct violation of civil rights, and was illegal under many different laws and documents. Among those documents was the Constitution. However, instead of standing behind the Constitution as they did when it came to issues of gun reform, Republicans claimed that this type of behavior was necessary for the safety of this country.

Notably, Texas Senator John Cornyn spoke out in favor of such illegal wiretapping. He said that it was a way to better understand terrorists that may be planning to harm the nation. He said that said that collecting phone call information was a necessary part of creating a web of safety and well-being for the American people. Let's follow this line of thinking. It is ok to ignore the Constitution when it comes to violating basic human rights, but not ok when you need to have access to guns. Right. This is a blatant case of supporting two different factors that both harm human life, while directly opposing measures that could be taken as a way to save lives. The statement was made by Cornyn back in 2006, right around when the NASA tapping was coming to light. He defended going around the Constitution, and stated that there needed to be exceptions for certain acts. However, seven years later in 2013 when the he was asked about the controversy behind guns, Cornyn stated that the Constitution was ironclad and could not be ignored. Seems pretty convenient.

One of the biggest problems with this argument goes even beyond picking and choosing when to follow the Constitution, it goes to the idea of safety. Overall, Republicans have supported wiretapping and surveillance on citizens in the past behind the idea that these methods could stop acts of terrorism. Another word they throw around a lot if "safe", as in keeping America "safe" or making sure that citizens are "safe" from terrorists. However, how much sense does it make to claim you are concerned with safety and then support the ownership of guns and restrict gun control laws? Guns are not simply dangerous; they are a device that claims lots of lives within America every year. Mass shootings from Americans kill more people in this great country of ours more than any terrorist attacks, and these shootings that are made more accessible due to the ability and readiness of guns. However, Republicans look over this problem when citing gun laws. They only care about the Second Amendment in the Constitution, and ignore everything else when they need to. This line of thinking doesn't make sense. They are willing to bargain away some of the most basic rights afforded to American citizens in the Bill of Rights under the guise of stopping terrorism, but will not do a thing to change the Constitution when it comes to limiting gun access or availability.

10. Wanting a Shutdown Without Any of the Blame

Once again, we are going to take a quick trip through history. However, instead of going back to a time where a group couldn't vote, or a time when George W. Bush was still gallivanting around the White House, we are only going back two years to 2013. In terms of government action, or lack thereof, 2013 was most notable for the government shutdown. This happens when the government quite literally shuts down due to a lack of cooperation between parties or sections of the government. This rarely happens, but can occur if things simply will not move forward in Washington. When this happens, many nationally run businesses and organizations all stop. As such, it is something that everyone actively tries to avoid. At least, that's what they say.

However, when the government did shut down in 2013, everyone was looking for something or someone to blame. As you can expect, the Republicans quickly pointed their fingers at the Democratic Party, claiming the party was responsible for the inaction that led to the shutdown. This took the blame away from the Republican Party and made it seem as if they were simply bystanders in an action that was otherwise out of their control. Yet, if you look at the statements many prominent Republican members made before the shutdown occurred (as we most certainly are) you will see a different story.

These statements go as far back as 2010, three years prior to the shutdown, and they all support the movement to bring the government to a standstill. Representative Mark Meadows is our first candidate for "largest proponent of a government shutdown".

In a letter Meadows wrote to Republican leaders, suggesting they tie the dismantling of the Affordable Care Act to the bill funding the government for the next year; a motion which would have stopped the government. Meadows even went as far as to convince seventy-nine of his colleagues to sign the letter, and got forty lawmakers to demand that the continuing resolution (the short-term government funding bill) zeroed out funding for President Obama's signature domestic policy achievement. Though Meadows claimed his point was never a shutdown, just to oppose the bill, it is clear where his intentions lay.

Next up is Texas Representative Steve Stockman, a man who had been ready to shutdown the government since August of that year. In a statement, he was quoted saying. "One of the things that we're doing wrong is that we're accepting the argument that when we defund Obamacare, that we're closing the government down. We're not! In fact, we're saving the nation's future by not funding it." Tom Massie, a Republican from Kentucky, was quoted with a similar statement, openly advocating for a shutdown as well. He implied that he did not mind losing his Senate seat, and said he would rather be at home anyway. This does not exactly sound like people who were trying to avoid the shutdown like they claimed once it happened.

Indiana's Mike Pence and Iowa's Steve King were also big backers of a government shutdown if they did not get their way. Mr. Pence, due to being moved to Indiana's Governor in 2012, is no longer in Congress. However, during his time in the seat he openly opposed the idea of abortion, and moved to have the government shutdown because of it. When asked if he was ready to shut down the government over such an issue he responded with "Well, of course I am." On the other hand, King has been very open about his attentions, calling for a government shutdown for years. This started in 2010, where King asked for a "blood oath" that The Affordable Care Act (also known as "Obamacare") would be repealed regardless of what it took, even if a shutdown was necessary. King said, "I'd like to challenge them to make that pledge." 2010 was a busy year for Republicans calling for a shutdown, and at that same time, Senator Mike Lee also made comments backing such action. While he was more sympathetic than his colleagues, stating that such moves were "frustrating", he agreed that a shutdown would most likely be necessary.

The final two quotes regarding the shutdown are from Tim Walberg from Michigan and Louie Gohmert from Texas. Both of these men backed the idea of a shutdown, and said it was "more than a possibility" due to Obama's policy. However, each of these men were also very opposed to the shutdown after it occurred, even demanding the blame be placed solely on Obama. All of these statements reveal hypocrisy about those events and how, even though they were opposed to it, each of these people supported the shutdown long before it occurred.

11. Protect Americans Overseas, Not at Home

Ever since the events of September 11th, the protection of America and its people has been the forefront of both foreign and domestic policy. Things such as the Patriot Act and the Iraq war have all been conceived in the same of protection. It is has been used as a fear tactic, a tactic to push agenda and, as with all political things, a tool. In terms of the Republicans, they have routinely pushed their own agenda in the name of "safety" and for the "protection of American lives". These are blanket words that sound nice in a speech, but really mean very little when compared to the actions of the party.

The biggest reason that such thinking is not actually what Republicans say it is, is due to exactly where and how danger comes from. This style of thinking seems to be based on convenience rather than fact. For instance, how the Middle East was only a threat to the people of this country once foreign oil became a necessity at home. Oh sure, Republicans care a lot about threats to American lives overseas, but they care very little for causes of death that happen on American soil every year.

For instance, let's talk about the subject of Medicaid. Expanding Medicaid is something that Republicans vehemently oppose, claiming that is a flawed plan in terms of both money and practice. However, estimates show that expanding such a plan would save around 17,000 American lives a year. 17,000. Yes, it is costly, but can you really say that there is a cost on American lives? True, there is no monetary gain from saving all of these people. However, if the interest of the Republican Party was truly in saving American lives as they have claimed so many times, they would put more support towards helping these people offset medical issues, not just complain about how it is costing them money. Politicians such as Rick Perry have repeatedly said that expanding Medicaid would be the same as adding a thousand people to the Titanic. That is, it would cause a lot more harm than good. However, just a little bit of research shows how absurd that sentiment is.

Another strange point surrounding Republican claims about American safety is their unwavering support to fund the war against ISIS. It seems that Republicans have a certain affinity when it comes to sending people to war, and this is no exception. They have pledged any funding necessary to get more control in the Middle East. However, as dangerous as ISIS is, you know what is even more dangerous? Heart disease.

Heart disease is one of the biggest medical problems in the United State today. A whopping 600,000 people die every year from heart disease, and one of the main causes of this disease is the consumption of red meat. A problem that could easily be fixed by limiting the amount of red meat Americans consume every year. However, whenever a proposal to place a limit on the consumption of red meat, the right wing has stepped up and shut it down in a pretty prime example of picking and choosing when to "care" about the lives of Americans. War? Good. Giving more funding and attention to medical problems that claim the lives of so many? Not worth the time.

This blatant hypocrisy can be seen over and over again throughout the current political agenda, and it permeates across multiple issues. When asked about ISIS, multiple Republican leaders have stated that we must do "whatever it takes" to combat the terrorist organization. They also said the same thing when it came to containing the Ebola outbreak in Africa. These are great statements, and show compassion for very important political issues. However, how much do these statements mean, when these same people, so concerned with the lives overseas, do nothing to tackle issues in America? Beyond blocking millions from gaining health coverage, they have also blocked gun control laws, and still maintain the idea that climate change does not truly exist. But who needs gun control anyway? Only 32,000 people die a year from firearms. Sure, that seems like a huge number that could easily be lowered through gun control, but you know what's more important? Taking on a terrorist organization thousands of miles away, to continue a thinly-guised war that will risk even more American lives.

It is not simply that foreign policy does matter, it does. However, there is a way to go about that without ignoring the thousands of Americans desperately in need of aid. There are many domestic problems, but since these problems are not in line with the Republican agenda, they are ignored entirely by the party. You can easily extend foreign policy under the banner of helping Americans, but if you don't actually help Americans, that statement means nothing at all.

12. Aid for My State, Not Theirs

Natural disasters are always hard. They can have huge ramifications on the state they affect, which can then spread out to the whole country. When such disasters happen, it is up to the government to make sure those states get the proper aid that they need. States that need aid should be allocated that aid when it is necessary. Unfortunately, this is not always the case, especially if you are a member of the Republican Party. Then you may think that certain states should get treatment over others; especially if you happen to be from that state.

The natural disaster we will discuss here will be Hurricane Sandy. Hurricane Sandy was particularly large weather storm that raged across the East Coast a couple of years ago. The rains and heavy winds barraged areas in many states, ranging across New York, Connecticut and New Jersey. As such, all of these areas desperately needed help in the aftermath of the disaster. Republicans did respond, but did so in a way that only accentuated the hypocrisy the party has continued to show.

Just as with helping Americans in certain situations, Republicans responded to the relief from Hurricane Sandy in a very selective way. True, they did seek aid for those who had been affected by the storm, but they pushed for aid in their home state before others. It doesn't take a genius to understand why this type of preferential treatment doesn't quite work when it comes to providing aid across a nation. In fact, many Republicans who rejected aid for those hurt by the hurricane actively asked for and proposed relief be sent to their own states. It should just be all or nothing.

During the ordeal, a bill was passed for such relief. However, this bill was voted against by 36 different Republicans. Not only that, but 31 of the Republicans who had opposed the measure had voted to support emergency aid efforts in their own states. They voted down all the aid efforts, including a much smaller $9 million bill that was put up earlier in the year. This would be fine if these men had stuck to their guns and went against all aid to Sandy relief efforts, but that is not what happened. Not even close.

While we will cover a slew of the no-voters and explain how their actions were just merely reflections of a hypocritical agenda, none are more ludicrous than the Republican senators Kelly Ayotte and Pat Toomey. While each of them voted against both bills, they had actually sought out disaster aid in their own states for relief from Hurricane Sandy. This meant they were lobbying for the exact type of aid they had voted against other states to have. This type of action makes no sense, and shows how self-centered certain people can be. In another crazy move, Senator John Boozeman from Arizona actually voted for snowstorm relief in Arkansas a mere four days before voting against efforts to help those on the East Coast.

The list of the no-voters is ripe with efforts of hypocrisy, and we will outline some of those efforts here in order to better understand just how two faced this party can be when it comes to serving their own needs.

We will start with John Barrasso, who requested disaster aid after flooding had occurred. Republican Conference Vice-Chair Roy Blunt demanded the Senate be called back from recess in order to pass disaster aid brought on from droughts. Richard Burr (R-NC) requested disaster aid after severe storms, and Saxby Chambliss from Georgia requested disaster aid after flooding occurred. Dan

Coats (Indiana) asked for disaster aid after tornadoes, and Tom Coburn (R-OK) requested aid after winter storms and for extreme drought. Pat Toomey, in a more extreme example, wanted disaster relief even before Hurricane Sandy hit landfall. This is a long list of examples, but it doesn't even come close to covering all of them.

Some more contradictory cases happened when Roy Blunt from Missouri called the Senate back from recess so that relief could be provided to his state following a massive drought. However, he voted against Hurricane Sandy relief. John Boozman of Arkansas asked for relief after severe snow storms in January 2013, and he too voted against Hurricane Sandy relief. Bob Corker of Tennessee asked for help following severe flooding in his state, and also he voted against relief. These three moves outline a very important snapshot of the party. It is alright to seek aid for oneself, as in the case of Paul Ryan and Social Security, but anyone else is up the creek without a paddle. This self-serving mentality runs through many Republican arguments, as we will see when we move further into the guide.

13. Taking Credit Where Credit is Not Due

One of the biggest elements of hypocrisy that we have not covered yet is not saying one thing while doing something completely different, or even stretching out the meaning of a certain phrase to sound better in a certain light, but rather, taking credit for something that you do not deserve credit for. This happens so often in the Republican Party it should be one of their trademarks just like guns and "Pro-life" are. The list of Republicans taking credit for things could probably fill this entire guide by itself, and in a way it does, but this section will be focused on a couple of key instances that best exemplify this point.

The first issue is the subject of Obama's stimulus plan. Opposing Obama's plan for reform has been at the forefront of the Republican agenda since he first took office. Obama has repeatedly slammed the party for their actions surrounding the stimulus plan, which was to reject it as much as possible, but then take credit for any actions from it that helped out their own constituents. Republicans have a lot of trouble understanding that you cannot have it both ways – either you're for or against the bill. In another example of Republicans directly refuting their own statements when needed, Republicans praised the stimulus plan in certain aspects, and took credit for a lot of the positive benefits that came from it. This had Obama very upset, and rightfully so.

Don Young from Alaska was one such Republican who was more than happy to take as much credit as he could for the same package that he so vehemently opposed. In a report, Young was quoted saying that the bill "was not a stimulus bill, it was a vehicle for pet projects, and that's wrong". Yet, he also took a lot of credit for the boost that the bill had for small businesses in Alaska. Young targeted a provision from the stimulus bill that would have required competitive bidding for grants and contracts. He got this provision pulled from the bill, and got the support from many people as a result

Geoff Davis of Kentucky was another man who went against the bill with all he could muster. That is, until he found ways he could benefit from the package. Eleven months after the stimulus package went through Davis touted a victory that the Carroll County School District was awarded a $1 million grant. Not only did he not mention Obama was directly responsible for these funds, but he actually took credit for the funding himself. He responded that his office was the one to secure the funding and, later that same day, issued a statement talking about the "failed" stimulus bill. So, what is it? Did the bill fail, or did the schools get the $1 million? It can't happen both ways.

Another representative who decided the bill was good after he had spent time trying to get it shut down was Bill Shuster. Shuster is a Republican out of Pennsylvania, who spent a lot of time speaking out against the bill. He claimed that the bill would hurt the economy, and bring about much more harm than good. In a seemingly (which happens to be the key word here) unrelated incident, Shuster attended and backed a ceremonial groundbreaking for a new facility as a sewage treatment plant in Blairsville. How did this great new plant get built? You guessed it. It was partly funded by money that came directly from the stimulus package.

When the bill was being touted, Phil Gringery was another opponent, saying that the plan would do nothing to help the American economy. In fact, he said the increased spending would just "bury future generations in more debt". That sounds like a man with a solid stance on this matter, but if we have learned anything so far, is that Republicans are not known for their steadfast idealism. Sure enough, Gringery took credit for helping the people of Cedartown, Georgia pay for new sidewalks, landscape and other improvements. The money, which totaled $625,000, came, similar to Shuster's treatment plant, right from the stimulus package. One last example, Richard Burr of South Carolina, voted against the package, but took $2 million of the money to erect a new fire station in Bethlehem Community Volunteer Fire Department.

Republicans may have problems with government reform, but they sure have no problem being a part of the reform when things go well. They also have no problem reaping the benefits from the reform as well. This goes for even when they are wrong (such as about the effectiveness of the stimulus package) or when they do not want to admit they are taking credit for something that was not originally their idea.

14. Background Checks on Voting, Not Guns

Ah, guns. This is not the first time, nor will it be the last, that we discuss the dangerous weapons. Republicans have long been huge proponents of guns, claiming things such as the 2nd Amendment for reasons they should be widely available. Yes, this does directly ignore statistics such as deaths related to firearms, but reason doesn't matter, all that matters are guns. Now, that argument aside, guns are a right, that is true. However, if you want to create gun reform that might lower the deaths related to guns while still making them available, that's too far. For Republicans it is either all or nothing, especially in the point of this section: background checks.

Republicans believe that guns are a right that should be afforded to any American who can legally purchase a firearm. They also believe, in this same vein, that such purchases should be a little more relaxed by not enforcing more background checks on those who are buying guns. This is a fine policy for anyone who isn't concerned with safety, but if that's your stance then fine, background checks are not necessary. However, Republicans don't actually feel that way. In fact, they think that sometimes, background checks are quite necessary.

Republicans have shown time and time again they believe that there need to be tighter voter I.D.. laws. If these restrictions were to be put in place, conveniently, many voters (most of whom are Democrats) would no longer be able to vote. This would actually affect a large majority of Americans, and keep them away from the polls. On the surface, voter I.D. laws seem to make sense. They are in place to keep voter fraud to a minimum. That's good, right?

Republicans would like you to think so, but it actually gets a little trickier than that for two distinct reasons.

One, voter fraud is basically non-existent. This was studied in Wisconsin, and found that only .00023% of the votes are the product of voter fraud. This number is so low, that there is a greater chance that a person is going to be struck by lightning than they are going to commit voter fraud. As such, what sense does it make to enact voter restrictions laws, when the problem they are supposed to fight doesn't exist? More importantly, if these laws aren't stopping voter fraud, what do they do? Well, they limit exactly who gets to vote. As you can imagine, most of the voters who are hit by the laws fall into three categories; low-income, colored people and students. It should then also not come as a surprise that all three of these demographics tend to vote democrat more often than not. Voting rights acts, which are laws in place to help create a fair, diverse voting environment, are in place to make sure this type of thing doesn't happen. Even so, Republicans are working hard to make sure these restrictions are in place.

On the flip side, while the Republican Party is so diligent in making sure I.D. and background checks are needed for voters, they seem to turn the other way when the idea of those same I.D. laws are being used for gun control. The biggest argument here, which once again cleverly ignores all of the data at hand, is that people are going to break the law with or without guns, so why punish law-abiding citizens? There are many holes in this argument, namely that restricting access to guns would indeed reduce the number of deaths per year. However, the real point here is, why background checks only need to be in place for parts of the equation that Republicans don't like.

In light of shootings that have happened in recent years, such as Sandyhook and Newtown, many have called for bills to pass in order to enforce more background checks on guns. However, time and time again Republican officials have stepped up to make sure these bills don't pass. This makes almost no sense when those same people are working as hard as they can to try and create voter restrictions. One such person is Senator Chuck Grassley from Iowa. Grassley has said that stricter background checks on guns are largely a frivolous endeavor, as shootings such as the one at Newtown would still have happened. Yet, he is also a very big proponent of limiting who can and cannot vote.

All of these statements lead to one simple, though ridiculous, conclusion; Republicans think voter fraud (which happens rarely if ever) is more of a threat that something that takes tens of thousands of lives a year. There is no doubt that expanding background checks would not be able to prevent every crime, and there is no data to suggest exactly what their effect will be. However, it is an accepted fact that the focus of the efforts should be consolidated onto the topic of American lives rather than whether or not a fraud vote slips through here or there.

15. Just a Few Glitches

Just when you thought Republicans would run out of things to complain about, or just when you thought they might take some time to relax or stop worrying about Democrats secret plot to ruin the world, they come back stronger than ever. This is mostly due to the fact that they have had a ton of problems with the way that Obama's people handle their policy, especially when it comes to the internet.

When the Affordable Care Act, something that Republicans already didn't want coming to fruition, rolled out, it also came with a website. A website was how the system was going to be implemented across the United States. However, as can be expected with any new technology, especially as one as massive as was planned for the Affordable Care Act, there were some glitches. This happens with any new website in the world, from the smallest to the largest. As such, it was bound to happen here. When hundreds-of-thousands of Americans attempted to enroll in a new online government health care program, they expected the government website to be perfect because it was touted as an easy way to study and choose the best option for their situation. However, there were "glitches", errors, slow response times, and the site crashed. This elicited frustration and anger, which prompted government officials to respond to complaints from prospective customers with promises to quickly assess and fix the problems. However, Republicans and the GOP didn't see it that way. No, they used these small glitches as fire to attack Obamacare as well as the entire policy.

When the glitches first occurred, Republicans immediately wrote off the entire project, labeling it as a failure, a classic overreaction that was simply people trying to make mountains out of molehills.

Kristen Powers, a contributor on Fox News, even went so far as to say the Obama Administration only had one chance to get the website right. She went on to say, "If the government can't build a functioning website to support the most important initiative of the president's administration, then how can it be trusted to do anything?" According to her, since it was not working perfectly right away, it was over, and the whole thing was lost.

However, before looking into this small (and easily fixable) problem, Republicans should have looked back into their own past before passing judgment. Of course, that's too much to ask, so we'll do it ourselves. Back in 2006, the Bush administration attempted to do a rollout. Here, it was Medicare Part D, and it was supposed to be expanded online. However, the release did not go smoothly, and there were more than a fair number of glitches in the system when it was first implemented. Did Republicans get mad then? Did they cry out at the "one shot" the Bush Administration had to get their policy right? Of course not. What did they do instead? Rather than criticize Bush in the same way they are criticizing Obama, Republicans urged the American people to be patient so they could, wait for it...sort out the glitches. When Bush and his people had glitches, it was ok, but when Obama has glitches for the exact same thing, it is a catastrophe.

In fact, when the rollout first happened, not only did Republicans not get angry, but Representative Joe Barton of Texas said of the Bush glitches, "This is a huge undertaking and there are going to be glitches." Republican representative, Tim Murphy (PA) also asked for patience, saying "Any time something is new, there is going to be some glitches. All of us, when our children were new, well, we knew as parents we didn't exactly know everything we were doing and we had a foul-up or two, but we persevered and our children turned out well." He even went as far as to discuss that it was going to take a little adjustment to get it right. Representative Nathan Deal of Georgia said that the glitches would be fixed over time, so there was nothing to worry about. Where was that same lookout with Obama?

Eventually, after the initial launch of Medicare Part D, the pitches were patched and things ran more smoothly. Reports showed that it ended up working well, despite the initial snafus. Even when things were not going smoothly, Democrats were quiet. They did not complain or lambast any of the problems that had arisen, nor did they criticize Bush. However, always the aggressor, the Republicans did not give Obama the same luxury. Even after, when the bugs were also sorted about for ACA's website, there was still some opposition. There is a clear double standard going on here, something that rests at the center of all hypocrisy, and the way the Republican Party handled these glitches is a prime example. Do something wrong under the Republican banner, and it is ok, mistakes happen. Make that same mistake as a Democrat? There is no forgiveness or understanding.

16. Maximum Wage, Minimum Effort

While all of the topics in this guide are very important to America and its people, wages are something that may be even more pressing. This is because wages directly affect people's well being, and their overall quality of life. Money is important, and it is one of the driving factors behind today's society. It is an old adage that money is power, but it is even truer that controlling money gives rise to even more power. Republicans know this, and they have tried to control money through constant restrictions on the national minimum wage. How is this hypocritical? Because, while they are so intent on stopping wage rises for the poor, Republicans have no qualms about not inflicting those wages on themselves.

Let's start with Rep. Lee Terry (R-NE) and his fight to increase wages...for himself. During the shutdown, Terry openly complained about his salary being frozen, and insisted that he did not make too much money. How much money does said Representative make? $174,000 a year. Pretty good, especially when one considers he does not work full time. That means that Terry made $1,794 every day he worked (assuming he didn't call in sick). However, ever greedy, Terry has reported that he wanted increases to his yearly salary, and even led the charge to give Congress an almost $5,000 pay increase in 2009. However, when a bill was proposed to increase minimum wages in 2013, Terry led a change with other Republicans to get it shut down. This clearly shows they believe the pay increases should only go one way.

Early in 2014, the Senate voted against passing another bill that would have increased the federal minimum wage from $7.25 an hour to $10.10 an hour. This was yet another rejection for legislation that had been a major focus for the Democrats' 2014 midterm campaign. Overall, the final count of the vote was 54 to 42, and minimum wage was stuck down. The bill needed to amass 60 votes to overcome a Republican filibuster of the bill. Democrats were only able to sway one Republican, Senator Bob Corker from Tennessee, to vote in favor of proceeding. Even if the measure had passed in the Senate, the chances that a minimum wage increase widely opposed by the GOP could make it through the Republican-run House of Representatives this year seemed improbable. This statement made it obvious what the Republican Party thinks about hard-working Americans, as shutting this bill down took away wage increases for almost 28 million Americans all across the United States. This bill would have even increased pay based on external factors such as inflation. Democrats were outraged by the bill's failure, and vowed to keep fighting for wage increases moving forward.

This above example was also not the first time Republicans have opposed increasing the minimum wage; this is something they have been fighting against for years, while keeping their own pockets quite full. In 2013, a similar bill was proposed that was focused on slowly increasing the federal wage to $9 an hour. As expected, Republicans managed to shut this bill down just as they did with the other one in 2014. The act would have also helped those trying to find jobs beyond just pay increases. It would have also eliminated or consolidated 35 federal programs, and created a Workforce Investment Fund to help those searching for a job to acquire the skills needed in order to join or integrate themselves into the workforce. However, just as with raising wages, those things just don't seem to be important to Republicans. More than 100 House Democrats also tried to get a bill passed for raising the minimum wage in 2012 as well, and also, this effort was shut down.

A good number of all of these no-votes came from Republicans, who claimed that such increases would hurt businesses, and do very little to take away from poverty levels. They claimed that, due to this, the extra spending on these programs in not justified. However, what is not justified is people like Terry not taking cuts from their own high salary like some Senators have done. And, if these wage increases are truly not important, it begs the question: if these claims do nothing for poverty levels, and such wage increases have no impact, then why are Republicans so insistent on increasing their own salaries? It is most likely because money does matter, and wage increases would mean a lot to millions of Americans. A lot more than an extra $4,000 means to a senator making five times the national poverty line.

17. Small Government Sometimes

Ask any Republican nominee, and they will tell you that being anti-government is a strict part of their policy as well as a basis for many of their beliefs. However, this turns out not to be true. As with so many of their so called "beliefs" and "policies" Republicans only follow certain stigmas for two reasons. One, when it supports their current agenda, or two, when it happens to align with the current voters. When it comes to being anti-government, they only want the government to stay out of their own issues, or things they need to get passed. However, when it comes to things they don't like, not only do they want the government to get involved, they want the government to create outright reform.

For example, the idea of low government interference is a policy that makes sense; letting more local and state levels handle their own laws. It sounds good on paper, and works for anyone running for a campaign under a banner that has long preached these ideals. Yet, when it comes to certain things like abortion or gay marriage (issues that Republicans are very opposed to) they want the government to be as involved as possible. Why? Because big government is the best way to make sure that these issues are restricted. However, when something like gun control comes down, it's all small government from there on out.

It is very obvious how contradictory that mindset is, but it does not stop Republican politicians from running on a strict "small government" platform. Even if it is just a myth, these claims are still being made on political platforms, and the worst part? People believe them.

One key example of this comes from a statement made by Republican Senator Tom Tillis from North Carolina. He touted about "small government" in his plan, when he discussed regulations that required businesses to make sure their employee's hands were washed after using the restroom. This makes sense; it's a good law and prevents many things that most people generally don't want around their food, such as disease or bacteria. However, it appears that Tillis, in all of his wisdom, does not feel this way. In fact, he said that such regulations should not exist, and businesses should be able to opt out of these regulations. Why? Because of small government, of course. Never mind the spread of disease, never mind the bacteria that could foster, it all comes down to the fact that the government should not be able to involve in small, private matters. Except when it involves abortion or gay marriage, then small government shouldn't exist. That argument holds no water.

Furthermore, if the market was truly "free" as so many people claim they want, then restaurants would have to also let customers know that employees did not wash their hands. As such, the entire argument goes nowhere. The whole ludicrous policy comes down to this. If you want the government to be small, then the government should be small and your policy should reflect that. If you want the government to be big, then it should be big and you policy should reflect that. Regardless of what all of these politicians say during their runs, it really is just that simple. However, the right goes takes this contradictory thinking just a little too far. The hypocrisy here lies in the fact that he wants to replace one government regulation with another completely pointless regulation, putting focus on things that don't matter, while ignoring the things that do.

18. Executive Inaction

This next section will cover a topic that is very much in line with the above section. In exploring Republican hypocrisy, we have looked at and discussed many different ways Republicans have managed to twist issues or events to make their own viewpoint seem correct. They did this with the idea of "small government" when they needed to use it to support their own motives, and they also have done this the idea of executive action.

Executive action is a very important part of the presidency. It is a directive issued to federal agencies, department heads or other federal employees by the President of the United States under his statutory or constitutional powers. It is one of the key elements that gives the president power, and enables him some control of what happens in this country. In this way, he can make things happen (or not happen), such as acts related to immigration.

We have already covered immigration in some detail, but here we will explore it more by looking at it through the lens of President Obama's own executive orders. In terms of vetoes, Obama has issued very little, relative to other presidents who have served in office. During his time in the White House, Obama has only vetoed two bills. This is a very small number when compared to someone like Franklin D. Roosevelt, who vetoed 635 bills over his 12 years, or even a President like Bill Clinton who vetoed 37. However, much to the chagrin of the Republican Party, Obama does have power, and this is where the executive orders come in. He has used these repeatedly, especially since a Republican-dominated Congress has largely blocked most of his domestic agenda. Past presidents have used this power, such as Ronald Reagan who issued 381 Executive

Orders compared to Obama's 200. Of course, facts such as those don't matter to the Republicans who have repeatedly criticized Obama's orders. George W. Bush even issued 291 Executive Orders, but no one took up arms against him.

Another issue related to hypocrisy surrounding this issue comes from a bill Republicans tried to pass on immigration. This bill was headed by the Speaker of the House John Boehner (R-OH), who had no choice but to cancel the vote on the border legislation after he didn't have enough votes to pass it. How did he respond to such a failure? By asking – no demanding – in a press conference that Obama to use his executive action to act alone and make sure the bill passed. The statement said that the House is useless, so the president needs to act alone on the border crisis. Not only does this line of thinking not add up, with Republicans wanting Obama to act on his own as a way to push their bill, but then call him a tyrant when he uses his power for other matters, but these allegations came right after the Republicans had voted to sue Obama for his use of executive power while in office.

The lawsuit is a ridiculous overreaction to hating Obama's policy. Not only, as we have covered, did the president not use his executive action in the past, but you cannot claim that Obama is evil or a tyrant and then turn around to ask him for the very thing that you are chastising him for. It isn't just that Obama should put an end to the so called "border crisis", but that he should use his "overused" executive action to do so.

This is one of the most blatant examples of hypocrisy in this guide, and the absurdity of it was noted by both liberals and conservative alike. This move was so insane, that even Fox News' Charles Krauthammer spoke against it, showing disarray inside the

Republican Party. It is ridiculous to sue the president on a Wednesday because he oversteps the law, as he has done a dozen times illegally and unconstitutionally, and then on a Thursday say that he should overstep the law, contradict the law that passed in 2008 and deal with this himself.

During this entire fiasco, Rogers also said that Obama should use his power responsibly to stop the crisis. This move was so bold, and such an over-the-top example of hypocrisy, that even their own people were turning on Republicans. This act confirms that Republicans only think that President Obama is a tyrant when he is doing something that they disagree with. When they need his help? He is just another ally.

19. Social Security for No One (Unless I Need It)

Another topic that Republicans like to flip-flop on is Social Security. You will find, or have already noticed, that many of the issues in this guide are things that have both good and bad properties. Not every political issue is going to be wholly good or wholly bad, and it is going to have benefits as well as downsides. That is the nature of the world. Republicans recognize this about Social Security, which we will explain below, but instead of admitting that, they seek to try and wage a war on Social Security instead.

Social Security is at the top of the Republicans list for things to abolish, and they have been going after it very hard for some time. This rose once Republicans had control of both houses. In January, the Republican Party included a new rule in their new rules package for governing the 114th congress. This rule seeks to prevent Congress from authorizing routine reallocation of funds to both the retirement and the disability program. So, if you don't fall into either of those categories, no big deal. However, for the millions of Americans who fall into those categories that could be a problem. Still, this new move also doesn't really affect corporations, so it's not a big deal to our money- loving friends in the Senate.

This is clearly a careless act and holds no regard for the lives of real people in the real world, but where does the idea of hypocrisy come into play? The hypocrisy of this sections stems from many of Social Security's biggest opponent's actually gaining benefits from the programs that they have vowed to abolish. One of these people is Paul Ryan, a Republican who served as the United State Representative for Wisconsin's 1st Congressional District since 1999 and as a Chairman of the House Budget Committee since 2011. He even went as far as being a candidate for the Vice President in the 2012 election. As such, you could say he is pretty popular and pretty involved with the party. In fact, one of Ryan's claims to fame was his direct and passionate opposition of the entire Social Security system. But that's not the whole story. Sadly, it never is.

When Ryan was 16, his father unfortunately passed away from a sudden heart attack, a very crippling event that would hinder a lot of families. This was particularly hard on Ryan's family, as it left his mother, three older brothers and sister alone. However, Ryan was under 18 at the time of his father's death, and was able to gather Social Security. This extra money helped him continue his life. In fact, he stashed away the checks and then wisely saved the money for college. Those extra funds are actually what allowed him to continue his schooling. This is a perfect example of Social Security being used for its intended purpose. The system exists in order help people stay afloat or keep on living through extremely hard times. When Ryan lost his father and needed a way to keep on living, Social Security stepped in and gave him that opportunity. However, years later it seems that Ryan has forgotten how much the money did for him, or what opportunities he gained from its existence.

If Ryan had never been able to receive Social Security, or if the system was not in place like he and so many from his party wish, then where would he be today? Of course, he no longer needs Social Security; he already got what he wanted from the system, so maybe it doesn't need to be in place anymore. Except, there are still millions of Americans (once again bringing up if Republicans truly care about "Pro-life") who need access to such funds to give them a way to stay afloat just like it did for a young Paul Ryan.

Another Republican who is against social programs is Dr. Ben Carson. He is a potential Republican candidate for the 2016 season, and hates the system along with everyone else in his party. However, Carson is even a little more extreme, as he is opposing care programs despite the fact that his own mother had to go on welfare. This is just another example of these programs being used by Republicans who so obviously and publicly speak against their very existence.

Social Security is blasted by people who say it serves as an entitlement that people using it don't deserve. There is no telling what Ryan would say if asked about this topic, since he wasn't "entitled" when his father suddenly suffered a heart attack. The reality is, the system is in place to help Republicans and Democrats alike, and Republicans only have a problem with that sentiment when the program is helping others who aren't them.

20. Temporary Job Creators

We have spent a lot of time discussing ideas or high, overarching political agendas. While that is all well and good at showing the obvious hypocrisy that exudes from the ideals of the Republican Party, here we are going to go over a more concrete example. Instead of looking at ideals or certain systems, we are going to discuss a pipeline. However, not just any pipeline. No, we are going to discuss the Keystone Pipeline, and how the reasons that Republicans have for funding or pushing this pipeline are not only flawed, but they just plain don't make sense.

The Keystone Pipeline, also known as the Keystone XL Pipeline, is a pipeline that is set to run 1,179 miles from Texas all the way to Canada. Senate Majority Leader Mitch McConnel of Kentucky even put this as the first thing he put to a vote when he took office in January. As such, it is plain to see how important this pipeline is for the oil industry. However, ultimately the creation of such a pipeline, due to the fact that it crosses International borders, is in the hands of the State Department, who have been reviewing its progress for six years. McConnel has stated that this project would create jobs, and even referred to the bill as "a very important job-creating bill". He, along with the Republican Party has opposed opposition to the pipeline in the names of hardworking, job-seeking Americans.

However, Republicans are using, as they so often do, such hardworking Americans as a way to get their agenda passed. Tens of thousands of new jobs from the construction of the pipeline would be great. It would employ many Americans, and give them nice, steady pay. If only it were true. The main problem behind the plan of the Keystone XL Pipeline is that it is only a temporary fix, not an end all like the Republicans are claiming it is. It is true, when the Pipeline first begins its construction straight through this beautiful country, it would manage to create 42,000 temporary jobs. Wait, temporary? That's right. This numbers looks great on paper, and even sounds good when being spoken on TV, but that figure of 42,000 people suddenly being employed would only last for so long. Then, you might ask, what happens after the pipeline is done? They would all go back to the same situation they are currently in. However, the Republicans would have their pipeline, so what does it matter if all those people are unemployed?

So, how many jobs will this brand new "job-creating" bill actually make? Thirty-five. That's right; only thirty-five permanent jobs would come from the pipeline. While this is a number bigger than zero, which is always good, why go to all the trouble to lie about job creation? Because Republicans have no problem skirting over trivial things (like the truth) when it comes to their own reports. Even looking at the temporary jobs, of the total 42,000, approximately 10,400 seasonal positions will only last for four to eight months. When you look at that over the course of two years, Politifact explains, that only comes out to 3,900 "average annual" jobs. Even more so, most of the construction jobs in Montana, South Dakota, Nebraska and Kansas, the states through which the pipeline will pass, will rely on specialists brought in from out of state.

This gets even more absurd when you look at a statement made by TransCanada's CEO, Russ Girling, Girling further stretched the truth into an outright lie on ABC's "This Week" Sunday morning, claiming that the State Department called those 42,000 jobs "ongoing" and "enduring." As these jobs will only last for the duration of the pipeline (if that) it is hard to say that these jobs are either of those words. However, "temporary" is not a word that many people like to hear when it comes to job security, and it is also not a word that gets things through the Senate.

There are even more holes that exists surrounding the pipeline and its plan. The State Department review has found that Keystone would have no damaging effects on the environment. However, there have been multiple conflicts of interest surrounding that claim, such as local impacts of leaks and emitting more greenhouse gases into the atmosphere. Additionally, studies have also shown the pipeline, regardless of what is being reported, will do nothing to lessen the United States' dependence on foreign oil. It won't lower gas prices either. Some experts even suggest that this new plan could raise them.

While Republicans continue to tote a false idea about job creation, they resist an agenda that would actually create new jobs: renewable energy. This includes things such as wind and solar. These fields brought around 80,000 new jobs in 2013, which was great for the workers of America. However, many leaders are very hesitant when it comes to committing to these plans. If Republicans were actually interested in creating jobs, maybe they should give this whole climate change thing another look. Right now, oil is much more important to them than helping the environment or creating jobs that actually last. At least, if the Keystone Pipeline does pass, those 35 people will be happy.

21. Educating Republicans on Sex

Moving forward, let's talk about sex. Sex is a fairly straightforward topic for anyone who is not involved in politics. It is a natural occurrence, and something that happens between two people. However, Republicans don't feel that way. They think it is best to restrict sex whenever they can. Instead of fostering progress by teaching or allowing people (mostly teenagers) to learn about sex, they try to hide it away and place restrictions on sexual education. This most specifically centers on abortions, and the way that, as always, the sum of the argument's parts do not cohesively add up to the whole.

While this section will focus around sex and sexual education, it more centers on the idea of teen pregnancy. Teenage pregnancy has been a growing problem in America, but the Republican Party thinks that it is not worth giving their time or effort to. This came to a climax during 2011. During that time, a vote of 65-34, the Senate passed *S. 403*, which made it a crime to go around parental-notification laws by transporting a pregnant minor across state lines for an abortion. All this did was make it harder for teens who had become pregnant to get an abortion. In the same vein, just before this bill was passed, Senate Republicans banded together to reject an amendment proposed by Senator Frank Lautenberg, a Democrat from New Jersey. Lautenberg's bill would have reduced the very teen pregnancies at issue in the Republican's bill. This brings up a very important question, do Republicans want teenage girls to have children? Of course, their mobilization to reject abortions makes it seem that they are anti-abortion. However, also rejecting the bill that would have reduced pregnancies in the first place is very suspicious.

The reason for this is, these two conflicting plans deliver a mixed message. Republicans are saying that they do not want abortion to happen. However, what's the best way to make sure that teenage girls don't seek abortions? To try and make it so the girls don't become pregnant in the first place. However, in the eyes of Republicans, this is a non-issue, and abortion, not preventing pregnancy, is the only thing that matters. If this sounds like a mixed message, it's because it is.

Lautenberg proposed his bill as a way to increase knowledge about sex to teenagers, which could be in fact very important to stopping early pregnancies. In this, he stated that his bill was "A comprehensive approach to sex education, which includes both abstinence and information on contraception, is the proven way to reduce the number of teen pregnancies". Abortion laws or not, the Republican Party was rejecting the bill as a way to kiss up to the Religious Right. Referring to *S. 403*, he then summed up the entire situation by saying "If the Senate passes this punitive bill but fails to do anything about teen pregnancy, it would prove that this exercise is only a political charade and not a serious effort to reduce abortions". A very good point, but as always, the Republicans had a counter argument to logic.

This counterpoint came from Republican Senator Tom Coburn from Oklahoma. His response to this fairly obvious point was that abstinence, not education or awareness, was the most appropriate solution. Lautenberg's bill directly states that "The Secretary of Health and Human Services may make grants to States, local educational agencies, State and local public health agencies, and nonprofit private entities for the purpose of carrying out programs of family life education, including education on both abstinence and contraception for the prevention of teen pregnancy and sexually transmitted disease, and education to support healthy adolescent development". Yep, that's what it says. It doesn't just offer ways of helping teenagers better understand sexual development, but it gives different methods to foster this learning, and even supports teenage growth. As such, you can see why the Republican Party is so afraid of such a terrifying bill coming into reality. If we have learned anything so far, there is nothing Republicans fear more than open information.

The federal government currently does not fund comprehensive sex-education programs, despite the fact that 75 percent of parents say that, in addition to abstinence, sex-education should cover contraception and other forms of birth control. However, with such contradictory actions, it is hard to see where Republicans fare. Yes, abstinence is a surefire way to stop teen pregnancy, but it is not a realistic way to stop it. What Republicans fail to understand is that they need to grasp the reality of the situation rather than try to appease their religious constituents. If they want to reduce the rate of abortion, they need to take steps to prevent teenage pregnancy through more realistic means.

22. Harming Small Businesses Digitally

So far in this guide, you might have been wondering, if we have discussed so many things that Republican ideology is opposed to, how have we not discussed the idea of small business? Ok, maybe you weren't thinking that, but it is a pertinent question that has some real validity. As with any case, small business is not a subject that works on its own. Here, in order to reveal the problems with Republicans and small business, we will discuss the tricky subject of net neutrality.

Net neutrality is a topic that allows freedom of the internet. Yes, the internet is (as long as you pay your provider) already free, but there are forces at work trying to change that forever. For those who believe in the idea of net neutrality, it is a principle that Internet Service Providers should enable access to all content and applications regardless of the source. This would also mean that every provider would access the same content, and not be allowed to block certain products or websites. A world controlled by what type of service you pay for is not a world that many want to live in, but it could become a reality if net neutrality does not stay in place. Fortunately, Obama has been a gigantic supporter of net neutrality, calling it "vital to the American economy" and even going as far to say that it "increases our very way of life". However, as one might be able to imagine, regardless of how good net neutrality is, if Obama is for it, Republicans are opposed.

As part of a long-standing Republican crusade against net neutrality, Ted Cruz, a name that we have already seen in this guide, went as far as calling it "Obamacare for the Internet" in order to get others opposed to the idea. On the surface, this opposition actually makes sense, because it falls right in line with the Republican's inherent distrust of new government regulations. However, there is also something a little more hypocritical underneath the surface. There always is.

While net neutrality is something that no one wants, many could live with it. Small businesses are what suffer the most from it being taken away. This brings us back to the point laid out in the opening paragraph. Small businesses can only really compete in today's corporation-dominated market through the internet. It gives them a chance to grow, a chance to reach out to people that they normally would not be able to reach and, of course, it also lets them sell to more people as well. With so much competition these days, many small businesses can only exist because of a free, open internet. However, if this were to change, or if net neutrality were to go away, then these businesses would suffer. This is because, if big content providers such as Netflix or Hulu pay for a faster delivery channel, they would simply push out startups or any of the competition who does not have access to such speed. In this way, it creates a chokehold on the market and starves small businesses.

However, while the Republican Party has no qualms about speaking against Obama, his new regulations, or net neutrality, they do claim to support small business and the "working man". In fact, the "average American" is one of their most solid platforms and something they convey in a lot of their speeches. Hard to see how they can convey they want the best for small business owners, when they are trying to oppose a law that allows them to exist in the first place. Yes, net neutrality runs counter to the Republican's idea of a free market, but removing it will shut down small businesses trying to get a hold in the market.

As always, there are other issues at hand, most of which are because Republican's own reasons for shutting down net neutrality are deeply flawed and not exactly rooted in fact. They have claimed, beyond the internet being used to stifle innovation, that net neutrality will cause an increase of taxes. This is not true, as, while the Communications Act would make telecoms pay a 16 percent service fee, broadband providers would not have to pay a similar tax. There is also the argument of the creation of excess bandwidth, which would cripple download speed. This is not true either. Currently, the United States has the 31st fastest download speed in the world (just behind Estonia), but this is not because big companies are restricted from making their own deals. In fact, deregulation of the telecommunications industry has allowed big companies like Verizon and Comcast to divide up markets, and still our download speeds are not up to where it could be. As always, while Republicans make many claims about a topic, not only do these turn out not to be true, but they also show that Republican beliefs are vastly different from the things that they say.

23. Free Speech We Agree With

Any country, like America for instance, or society that is truly free hinges on one single element: the idea of free speech. Yes, there are always other factors at play, but free speech is one of the most important, and the gear at the center that turns the entire machine. However, free speech is a two-way street, and that is important to understand when discussing the ideals that come with free speech. Yet, it is true that can say whatever you want, but in exchange for that right, you also have to be ready to allow others to say whatever they want. This goes even if those opinions go against what you think, or if they clash with your own personal beliefs. It is this kind of thinking that fosters such a free-thinking society and allows thoughts, discussion and discourse to grow. Conservatives love punishing any human being that dares to hold or express an opinion contrary to their ideology, and that calls into question their advocacy for the right to speak freely; particularly when it involves religion or politics.

Once more, this section will look at Republicans that want certain rights and freedoms to only apply to those who follow their own beliefs, and not to anyone else. There is a pretty strong theme in this guide. One example of this comes from the Dixie Chicks, a popular band who was very outspoken about their feelings towards Bush. They didn't like him, and because we live in a country that allows anyone to speak their mind they didn't care who knew it. However, Republicans did care, and they fought back by slamming the chicks for their anti-Bush sentiments. This is fair, just as the Dixie Chicks were allowed to bash Bush; the Republican Party was allowed to bash them.

Flash forward to 2013, and this same situation came up again. However, instead of the Dixie Chicks getting attacked for their anti-Bush remarks, it was Phil Robertson of Duck Dynasty. Robertson came under attack for saying anti-homosexual and homophobic remarks that spoke out against the gay community. The backlash was so severe that A&E went as far as to cancel the show in response. Many were outraged, claiming the company had no right to do this. They also claimed that Robertson's opinions, while bigoted, were fair under the idea of free speech. This is true, these opinions are fine for him to have and, under the Constitution, he is free to express them. However, that does not mean that A&E cannot take action in response to those statements. Just as Robertson has the right to speak his mind, A&E has the right to protect their studio. Here is where people, Republicans in general, get confused.

Freedom of speech, while allowing you to say or speak your mind, does not make you immune to any action being taken against you. Freedom of speech, while not giving you total immunity, is exactly that, a freedom of speech. But just like you can boycott The Dixie Chicks if you don't agree with them, A&E was free to cancel Robertson's show if they felt he was misrepresenting their company. That's how this works. When Robertson signed his initial contract, it almost certainly included a clause to say that he is a representative of A&E and is expected to act accordingly. All public figures, whether they want to be or not, are representatives of something; be it a company, a brand, a sports team or league; it's the price that comes along with fame. This logic is sound, and accurately defends the themes of freedom of speech, but of course, there are some Republicans who do not quite agree. Of course, Robertson can't be jailed for his statements, but he can certainly suffer repercussions from his employer.

In a stunning act of both ignorance and hypocrisy, ex-Republican candidate Sarah Palin, made famous by her inane comments during the 2008 election, rushed to Robertson's aid. However, Palin also, shortly after defending Robertson, admitted that she had not read nor heard his comments before coming to his aid. In actuality, she just blindly defended him based on the information she had, rather than on anything that was based in reality. This is one snapshot in time, but it serves as a great example of how Republican thinking and mentality works for these types of issues. Ted Cruz and Louisiana Governor Bobby Jindal also rushed to defend Robertson. Even so, Robertson was, as predicted, suspended for his comments.

24. Occupy Congress

Occupy Wall Street, while starting slow, turned into one of the most substantial American movements of the 21st Century. It was a very diverse event that showed the power the masses have. It also acknowledged their displeasure with the upper classes. Yet, little of this mattered to Republicans, who actively came out and opposed the movement. This was mainly due to this movement attacking the wealthy, which many members of the Republican Party are, and how many of the party saw these protests as a threat to their luxurious lifestyle. While these beliefs held true across the party, one specimen who had his own reservations about the Occupy Wall Street movement was Eric Cantor.

While you may not be familiar with the name Eric Cantor, he is an American politician, lawyer and businessman who served time as the United States representative for Virginia's 7th congressional district from 2001 to 2004. Always on the side of his party, Cantor spoke publicly against the movement, and even went as far as to openly criticize it for things that didn't make any real sense. What were these arguments? First, Cantor was quoted calling the protesters "mobs", which was perfectly in line with the Republican Party's allegations that the protesters were simply unpatriotic, angry troublemakers looking to stir up problems. While these allegations were clearly not true, they were clearly at the forefront of Cantor's mindset when he moved against Occupy Wall Street.

Many of the things that Cantor said were during a time when he endorsed the Teabaggers for protesting health care reform, loss of liberty and taxes that were too high. In this same report he stated "believe it or not, some in this town have actually condoned the pitting of Americans against Americans". This sentence, we will quickly see, was his first mistake when trying to put together a cohesive argument.

While it may be nice to say things like "pitting Americans against Americans" without following truth or logic, the truth of it is, Republicans have been actively pitting Americans against each other for some time. And this goes far beyond simply supporting the Teabagger movement. It is one thing to be against the movement that was Occupy Wall Street, but it changes entirely when that movement is being called out for the very same things the person attacking it does. Republican movements to create a class divide in this nation show that Republicans criticizing Occupy Wall Street is the pot calling the kettle black.

A good example of this is Republican attempts to pit rich Americans (along with the corporations they feed off of) against the middle class and poor. This class war has been on the rise since Obama first took office, during which the Republican Party has made countless claims that Democrats (obviously not them or their own people) are killing jobs by overtaking and over-regulating the so-called "job creators". They even said that the new banking and health insurance reforms were the sole reason that high employment has taken hold in the sluggish economy. Not only is there no truth to these claims, but it also serves as a great example of hypocritical thinking.

Through propaganda such as the one referenced above, the party has been very successful at pitting ignorant Americans against other Americans who understand the GOP is only interested in the extremely wealthy. Beyond that, they couldn't care less. This is the main reason behind their adversity to Occupy Wall Street; it wasn't a movement that pitted Americans against Americans, it was a movement that threatened the rich Republicans from keeping their wallets full.

If Cantor was really concerned that Americans are being pitted against one another, he should cease and desist the Republican rhetoric that programs that benefit the majority of Americans is hurting the country. Republicans have forged ahead by decimating the poor, middle class, and seniors by slashing programs that benefit all Americans to give the wealthy, corporations, and the oil industry more entitlements. It is class warfare that pits the wealthiest 1% against the rest of the population.

While it would be nice if the above example was the only hypocrisy in this section, it most definitely is not. Republicans have also been trying to pit young Americans against the elderly as well. They do this by trying to convince those who do not know better, that Social Security and programs such as Medicare are killing the jobs on which the youth depend on. This is a lie fostered to try and push their own programs through. It also creates a class war the Republicans, not the folks who occupied Wall Street, want.

Finally, even if the movement did not sit well the Republicans, or even if it was a way to attack other Americans, it is perfectly protected under the Constitution. Let us not forget the little thing called the First Amendment that allows Americans the right to assemble peacefully. Since we learned in the subject of gun control that the Constitution is, and always should be ironclad, shouldn't the Republicans then be for these protests? Or, maybe the Constitution, just like the logic Cantor and his buddies use, is only for when the Republican Party need it to prove a point.

25. Who Really Killed Osama bin Laden?

Osama bin Laden. That is a name that George W. Bush, in his ongoing war for oil and power, made sure would ring with infamy for the rest of his life. It was a name associated with terror, with fear, and with some of the most brutal attacks to ever occur on American soil. Needless to say, he was a bad guy. His story came to a head in 2011, when bin Laden was finally tracked down and killed during a top secret Navy Operation that happened in the Middle East. This was due to many factors, but one of the largest was Obama's own determination and the expert planning of his staff. However, nothing good, not even hunting down one of the worst terrorists in recent history, can happen under Obama's watch without the Republicans having something to say about it.

This actually is quite impressive when you think about it. How on earth do you try and spin a story that was so plain and obvious. Osama bin Laden died under Obama's presidency and operations. That is a fact. That cannot be argued with. However, we know by now how the Republican Party feels about facts, and this was one of the most stunning displays of ignoring the truth that the party and its delegated have ever shown.

Soon after Osama was pronounced dead, Republicans quickly jumped on the bandwagon and tried to claim the credit. They did this by saying that Obama's actions would never have amounted to the killing of bin Laden without steps that George W. Bush had taken during his presidency. First off, this makes no sense, as the Republicans are usually trying to give Obama credit for things that Bush did, such as the Gulf Oil Spill, the weak economy, and the nation's deficit problems. It usually doesn't work the other way around. And yet, that's exactly what they were attempting to do here. Leading this charge was the Washington Times, who had reported that Obama gave no credit to Bush when discussing the capture and kill of bin Laden. Which begs the question, why give credit when no credit is due? The paper also went on to say that, without Bush, Osama would still be alive somewhere in the world.

On of the Republican favorites, Sarah Palin, also decided to weigh in on the issue. She claimed that it only made sense to thank Bush, due to the fact that Bush was the one who took actions that eventually led to Obama's victory. Not only that, but during her speech in Colorado when she discussed the event, she didn't even call out Obama by name. Rather, in a classic Republican move, she only spoke about Bush. Countless Republican sources, such as Breitbart's Big Peace and Fox, all attacked Obama for not giving Bush the credit he deserved (which was none) and ignoring the last President. This comes from a very interesting point of view, where, in the minds of the Republicans, Obama only takes credit for the things Bush did well, not the things he did wrong.

There have been many instances throughout Obama's campaign where members of the Republican Party have bashed the president for things that were both not his fault or in his control. In fact, they were Bush's. It doesn't take a Harvard degree or an incredibly smart mind to realize that Bush had some very bad policies all across his eight years. He put this country in debt, started a war with no end, created general turmoil, and even passed laws that challenged our basic civil rights. The biggest, and sorest, of these topics is the economy. Republicans have routinely liked to blame Obama for the state of the nation's economy without ever mentioning that it was something that Obama inherited from his predecessor. Republican golden child Rush Limbaugh even stated that Obama needs to own up to the fact that economy problems are his and his alone.

This is the ultimate problem with the entire bin Laden situation. It is not simply that Republicans are trying to give Bush credit for something that isn't his, but that they are attempting to make Obama take responsibility for Bush's actions. If you bring up the war in the Middle East or the weak economy, those don't fall on Bush; they are somehow only Obama's responsibility. However, if you try and say that Obama is only responsible for bin Laden, it is suddenly Bush's responsibility as well. You can't have it both ways, although Republicans will most certainly try. Either what Bush did during his presidency, the good and the bad, falls on Obama's shoulders, or it doesn't.

26. Fiscal Irresponsibility

One of the main standpoints of the Republican Party is that they proudly brand themselves as the party of fiscal responsibility. They love to say that they always look out for the economy, balance budgets, and can accurately take care of American's money (which would make sense since they control so much of it anyway). However, rich or not, this is not true. When going back into the depths of history and the history of the party, you can find their claims are completely and utterly laughable.

How fiscal is a party that has, time and time again throughout America's history, worsened the American financial situation. The last Republican President who managed to balance the nation's budget was Dwight D. Eisenhower. For reference, Eisenhower served during between 1953 and 1961, quite a long time ago. This is even more important when you realize that Bill Clinton paid off more than $360 billion in debt during his time in office. This came as a result of 115 straight months of economic expansion that began after an increase in the top income tax rate. This move was virulently opposed by the right, the huge deficits left by 12 years of Republican rule had been transformed into a surplus. Ronald Reagan also nearly quadrupled the national debt during his time in office. Bush doubled it during two terms.

Following Clinton's term, Bush then entered office and quickly turned the surplus into a deficit that continued to grow. During this time, Vice-President Cheney laughed off allegations that the Bush tax breaks would ultimately pay for themselves. In fact, he even said that "Reagan proved deficits don't matter". This implied that Republicans did not care about such deficits, but that is not always the case. In fact, tax breaks matter a great deal to Republicans; however this conveniently only happens when a Democratic President is in office. In this case, that President is Obama. The basis of most of their concern comes from allegations that he started the deficit, which of course came from Bush and choices made during his term that Republicans refused to abandon or give up. They also say that the deficit was responsible for the poor economy, but of course, it can be seen that this was not true.

Time and time again, Republicans have added to the national deficit. That is not the work of fiscally responsible people; it is the work of people who don't care about the national debt. This was most recently seen in 2014, where Republicans fought to pass a bill that would add $310 million to the deficit by making six permanent tax cuts to business. Not only this, the tax cuts would be completely unpaid for in addition to doing more harm than good. Economists have warned multiple times against unpaid tax cuts, as they will simply increase the debt. And, in conjunction with these warnings, many House Republicans have even said that the debt needs to be reduced. Yet, of course these pleas have fallen on deaf ears, and problems continue to mount.

To put how much $310 billion is into perspective, it represents half of the entire federal deficit this year. That is the lowest it has been President Obama took office. It's almost two-thirds of all non-defense domestic discretionary spending, more than three times what we spend annually on education, job training and social services; and five times more than we spend on medical research and public health. Also, five times more than we spend on the veterans Republicans don't care about. Moments before Republicans on the Ways and Means Committee voted to add $310 billion to the deficit, they objected to a provision offered by Committee Member

Lloyd Doggett (D-TX). That provision would have helped abused foster children find work, and would have cost only $1 million a year. Four month prior Republicans let emergency unemployment insurance expire for more than 1.3 million Americans (now 2.6 million) by arguing that an adequate offset had yet to be proposed.

How is it possible that a party that is so bad with money, a party that was so responsible for increasing the national deficit and bringing us into a dark age of economy, still considers themselves fiscally responsible? It doesn't add up, and is another baseless claim by the right wing. Just as was seen in the case of both free speech and big government, Republicans are saying something while not acting accordingly. They can tout their own manta about fiscal responsibility, but this only applies to programs they don't agree with. When they don't agree, they love spending giant heaps of money on programs they agree with, such as big oil subsidies, tax breaks aiding corporate welfare and giant defense contracts. Just because Republicans only spend money on things they want, doesn't mean they aren't spending money.

27. Canada is More of a State than Hawaii

Another (ridiculous) point of contention that Republicans have repeatedly made regarding President Obama is the fact that he is not a true American citizen. This statement, as so many Republican statements often do, makes very little sense. President Obama was not born in the Continental United States, but he was born in Hawaii. Now, if you didn't pay attention in history class (and it seems that many who made these claims did not) you may not know that Hawaii is a part of the United States. However, if you had any basic schooling, it is quite obvious that Obama is in fact a United States citizen. Ignorance has long been the tool of the Republican Party, and in this section we will explain exactly how absurd the heights of such ignorance can actually reach.

First things first. Obama's birth certificate states that he was in fact born in Hawaii. As such, he is an American citizen, and that should be the end of the conversation. However, as stated, this isn't so easy for Republicans. Many high-profile supporters of the Republican Party, such as Sarah Palin and Donald Trump, have made baseless claims surrounding Obama's birth. In these claims they accuse him of being from Kenya. Unfortunately for them, his birth certificate, which is a legal document, says otherwise. The "Birther Movement" has no basis in reality, and is just another bullet Republicans use to try and discredit the president. Yet, that same bullet could soon be the ones that Republicans use to shoot themselves in the foot. This is because Senator Ted Cruz, one of our old friends has once again, come back into this guide.

If Cruz does indeed to run for President in 2016, as many have speculated he might due to his popularity with the Republican Party, it would be hypocrisy of the highest degree. Cruz has many of the flaws and ignorant tendencies that Republicans tend to love. He fights their fights, wages their wars, and backs all of their opinions without worrying for the facts. And, much more importantly for the purposes of this section, he was also born in Calgary. Yes, Calgary. Not Calgary, Atlanta or Calgary, Oregon. No, Mr. Cruz, possible future Republican running candidate was actually born in Canada.

While it is nice to make baseless speculations about Obama's birthplace, and say that he was not born in this country, he actually was. However, Cruz was not. Is that going to matter to Republicans when or if he runs for President in 2016? Are they going to cry foul then? Highly unlikely. Much more likely, they will back him with everything they have. In this way, it is very easy to see how deep this ignorance runs. Republicans have routinely chastised Obama on false claims that he was not born here, but they are more than ready to back a candidate who actually was not.

Though he was born in Canada, Cruz's mother was American and his father was Cuban. As such, by the rules laid out in the Constitution, Cruz is still an American citizen. This allows him to run for president, and gives him the rights anyone else has. If he does decide to take a shot at office, will people stand up and try to make sure he can't? How will Democrats and Republicans be able to cope with the fact that the possible president of the United States was born across the northern border? Of course, these are absurd statements, but they do prove a very important point; which is that no one is going to question Cruz about his birth because it is pointless to do so. Republicans are questioning Obama's just to cause commotion and stir up trouble. Republican Congressman Blake Farenthold of Texas actually went as far as to promise to "take a look" at the claims regarding "the fraudulent birth certificate of

Barack Obama's". At some point, this just becomes offensive, and the claims don't even stop there.

Another congressman out of the great state of Texas, Steve Stockman, has also continued to question the president's birthplace. There is no doubt that such nonsense could quickly and easily by squelched by someone with as much power in the party as Cruz. However, it seems he is perfectly content to let these baseless claims and false information permeate around. Though, it does bring up a very good point about his own presidential run. If anyone were to step forward and question his citizenship, would he be so quiet then? Quite unlikely, as, if we have learned anything so far, Republicans never have any problems when the gun isn't pointed at them. It is only when it changes targets that they start trying to do something about it.

28. Black or White

In this section, we are going to talk about guns. Guns, again? Unfortunately, yes. Republicans love their guns, and go to great lengths to make sure they can both keep and own them. In fact, as we have already seen, they have been mobilizing for some time in order to make it easier to own a gun, and lower the restrictions on who exactly can purchase one. In their eyes, if you can breathe and are of legal age, you should be able to own a gun. This right is protected by the Second Amendment, but sometimes this love for guns leaks into other issues as well. Here, it leaks into the much more serious issue of race, more specifically: black and white.

We start with the events that took place in Ferguson, Missouri. Here, a young, black man named Michael Brown was gunned down by cops. It is the general opinion that the killing was an act of unnecessary violence, and that there was no reason behind it. However, we are not going to discuss the morality of what happened, we are going to exactly how this event reflects onto gun laws. After the events of Ferguson, not one pro-gun person stood up and came to his aid. One of the biggest arguments people make in support of the Second Amendment is that the public carrying guns is the ultimate defense against oppression. While we will cover this in greater detail below, this argument was nowhere to be found when Brown was gunned down. Not one head of the Republican Party supported that Brown should of had a gun to fight back against the police who took his life. In addition, no one also said that Trevon Martin should of also had a gun when he went to the store to get candy. All of the guns rights activists are happy to raise their voices when it comes to passing a bill through Congress, but when a kid is gunned down, none of them step up to say that those deaths could have prevented through the use of guns. Silence is often one of the most used tools of the Republican Party, and here is a classic example of why.

It always helps to put faces to problems. We will look at some more specific people who accentuate the hypocritical thinking and actions that seem to follow gun control laws. The first such person is Larry Ward. Ward is the chairman of Gun Appreciation Day, and a man who made of the most idiotic statements someone in office could make. He said that slavery, a topic it is very doubtful he has little to no right to speak about, would not have happened if African Americans had guns. This is, according to Ward, that guns are things that allow the common man to stand up and fight against oppressors. This, not political agendas, is the reason that Republicans fight so hard for gun access, at least so they claim. However, when African American kids are gunned down by police, Ward was nowhere to be found.

This gun hypocrisy even shows how sometimes conservatives and the right wing can even overstep the bounds of their own insanity. This happened during an incident that happened with a cattle rancher by the name of Cliven Bundy. In 2014, Bundy fought back against government officials using guns. In what has become known as the Bundy Standoff, he sought to settle a 20-year legal dispute between him and the United States Bureau of Land Management. This dispute was a result of unpaid grazing fees that developed into an armed confrontation between protesters and law enforcement. This seemed like a perfect example of what the pro-gun right Republicans spend so much talking about. The Bundy Standoff showed that guns can be used in self-defense or as a way to protect your property and livelihood when it comes under threat from the powers that be. In fact, many Republicans were quick to praise Bundy's actions and herald him as a hero. Though, that quickly changed.

This change was because, after being in the spotlight, Bundy made some very, shall we say, interesting comments about slavery. He was quoted saying that the "Negros" had been hurt by emancipation. His direct quote was that "They abort their young children; they put their young men in jail, because they never learned how to pick cotton,". As shocking as that is, he went onto say "And I've often wondered, are they better off as slaves, picking cotton and having a family life and doing things, or are they better off under government subsidy? They didn't get no more freedom. They got less freedom." A clearly offensive and absurd statement, and, as expected, many Republicans who spoke out to first back Bundy and his actions quickly changed their story. Senator Dean Heller was one of those people. After the initial incident, he heralded Bundy as a patriot. However, after Bundy came out as a pro-slavery racist, Heller's office stated that Heller completely disagreed with Bundy's statements. As always, this only came at a time where it looked good for Heller, and not whether it was right or wrong. Another example of how Republican outrage seems quite limited to circumstance.

29. Thankful for Low Gas Prices, But Not for Obama

Though most of the topics we have discussed in this guide have been polarizing in one way or another, here we will look at something everyone likes: low gas prices. Low gas prices are something that brings America together, something that everyone can agree on. It doesn't matter if you are a Republican or a Democrat, whether you are pro guns or against them, it is always a good thing when it costs a little less to fill up your tank. However, the confusion enters the equation when it comes to attributing credit to who exactly lowered such prices. Of course, while prices have lowered considerably during Obama's time in office, it seems the answer to that should be obvious. However, of course Republicans are not so quick to give Obama that credit. In fact, they even go as far to blame him when things don't go according to plan.

Before we can even begin to explore the hypocrisy surrounding the rising and lowering of gas prices, we need to talk about the gas market as a whole. Gas prices, while easy to attribute to those in the Oval Office, are not actually even close to in the president's control. Global markets and the world economy affect national oil. The availability and trade of said oil is what directly affects gas prices. Is any of this under Obama's control? No. Yes, there are many things the president can do from his chair, and some of those things might even have a small effect on oil, but gas prices are decided by factors largely outside of his reach. This is important to understand before exploring this topic, because it exemplifies how ludicrous the claims we are about to explore actually are.

The person who is at the center of this section is Republican House Speaker John Boehner. Boehner was very energized about the high price of gas in 2011, when prices were up to almost $4 a gallon. During a press conference, Boehner was very quick to blame Obama for the rise in prices. He cited Obama's moratorium on oil drilling in the Gulf as a reason for the spike, as well as the president's decisions to cancel leases on drilling in national parks. It should come as no surprise that Boehner did not mention the turmoil in the Middle East, which is the real cause behind the increased spike, during the conference. This is a classic example of ignoring the problem. Boehner condemned Obama's policy, but gave no light to the actual issues at hand. In fact, the White House even released a statement explaining that a lot of the rising prices were directly related to issues in Libya, but these went ignored.

Boehner did not care about this report. In his comments he said that "The Obama administration has consistently blocked America's energy production. They are imposing steep regulations on American businesses that are going to sharply increase the cost of energy." Boehner also cited Obama's reduction in the number of drilling leases and Environmental Protection Agency regulations that he believes hurt private companies. All of this makes a lot of sense on paper, if only any of it were true. However, as we have already covered, the global market, not government regulations, is what is affecting the long term oil and gas prices.

Gas prices have long been the catalyst for a very common debate between Democrats and Republicans regarding energy as well. On one hand, Republicans are quick to call for more off-shore drilling, while Democrats want to seek out more ways to develop alternative energy. During his attacks on Obama, Boehner took a breath to promise that at some point, Republicans will push energy legislation.

One example of this was a bill that he claimed would encourage royalties from oil and gas drilling to go toward renewable energy. A very nice gesture. However, words are simply words, and nothing really that goes beyond that. It is quite obvious that Republicans will say what it takes to appease the public; whether they actually do it is a different matter.

One more factor that must be mentioned is, amid all of the talk about rising gas prices and global economy, prices actually lowered late in 2014. This drastic drop came at a good time for all American consumers, and was very helpful during the holiday season. Boehner even weighed in, tweeting that everyone should be thankful for the lower prices. Yet, in this tweet, he did nothing to thank Obama. In fact, he completely ignored the fact that Obama's administration was the one who was in office during the oil drop. Of course, the lower prices were not a result of Obama, but if Republicans are willing to blame him for things that are out of his control, they should also praise him for such things as well.

It is not simply that gas prices are high or low, that's not what's important here. What's important is how quick Republicans are to blame the things they don't like, or things that go wrong, on Obama, but will not mention his name in any discussion when things go right. This is a very common theme in this guide, but no section really shows this type of flawed thinking in such a blatant way. Boehner can spout about prices all he wants, he can tweet all he wants, but if he is going to damn Obama for high prices, he should be thanking him for the low ones as well.

30. Is it Okay to be Gay?

Another tricky subject we have yet to cover is the subject of gay marriage. Oh, wait tricky is the wrong word. The right word there is "basic human rights" and "equal opportunity". However, the Republican Party can't waste their time with silly things like that. Rather, they try as hard as they can to make sure gay people cannot have normal lives in this country. The Republican Party has long taken a stance against gay marriage, and routinely tried to stop the gay community from getting married or being afforded the same rights as others. Whether you agree with these sentiments or not, as Robertson taught us during his A&E debacle, it is ok to have your own opinion. Where these actions becomes suspicious is that, so many of the Republicans who come out and take stances against gay marriage, either exhibit gay behavior, or turn out to be gay themselves.

There is a very long list of different Republicans who have been caught exhibiting such behavior. Of course, there is nothing wrong with this. However, due to the amount of time they have tried to stop gay people from reaching equality, it sure depicts a large amount of hypocrisy. We can start our analysis with former senator from Idaho, Larry Craig. Craig was a very large anti-gay supporter who supported the Federal Marriage Amendment, which restricted marriage to be legally defined as between one man and one women. He also supported Idaho's proposed ban on same-sex marriages. Those are pretty strong indicators that he is against gay rights. However, in 2007 Craig found himself in a compromising situation when he propositioned an undercover policeman in a bathroom at the Minneapolis-St. Paul International Airport by tapping his foot in a bathroom stall. After he was arrested, Craig of course denied he was trying to do anything sexual, but he did plead guilty to disorderly conduct. Whether you believe him is up to you.

Florida Representative Bob Allen followed in Craig's footsteps when he voted against gay rights in the Florida legislature, but was later arrested for offering an undercover policeman $20 for sex. He had used his powers to vote against gay rights multiple times in the Florida legislature. Also, he is married with three kids.

Another hypocritical Republican is former member of the Washington State House of Representatives, Richard Curtis. Curtis took his own stance on gay rights one step further than the two above men by, not only voted against including LGBT folks in the state's discrimination statutes, but he also voted against granting same-sex couples the rights of domestic-partnership. Even so, he "chose" to resign in 2007 (which seemed to be a big year for this type of activity) when he was caught in a motel-room with a gay male prostitute.

California is largely considered one of the most progressive states when it comes to gay rights, but Roy Ashburn was not a part of that trend. Ashburn is a Republican State Senator from California who directly voted against the gay rights measure when it was put before him. Yet, in 2010 he was busted for a DUI after driving away from a gay bar. Unlike many of the people in this list, Ashburn actually took this opportunity to come out as gay, rather than try and make excuses for his behavior. This was a far cry from Ed Schrock, who rather just resigned from his running for a third term as a Congressman in Virginia when he was caught soliciting gay sex on a gay sex phone line.

Each of these men renounced their own sexuality in order to keep in line with their party. It should come as no surprise that list is quite short, and there are even more in the Republican Party who have been accused or are largely expected of this behavior. Patrick McHenry is one of them. McHenry is a Republican Congressman from North Carolina who has supported the idea of putting an anti-gay amendment in the Constitution. Those are pretty strong feelings for a man who bought a house with a male companion. But it doesn't stop there. Charlie Crist, the governor of Florida, has been accused of engaging in gay sex by multiple men despite the fact that he has supported both a ban on gay marriage and a ban on adoption by same sex couples. Of course, all of these are just speculator examples, but given the repeated denial seen within the Republican Party about such allegations, it is not out of the realm of possibility that they could turn out to be true. Denying gay rights is so often done by those who are gay, that is almost a red flag by this point.

There is nothing wrong with these acts, but a common thread of secrecy and shame runs through all of the above examples. It is not simply that these men are gay, but they choose or are forced to hide their sexuality as a way to make their platform better. Renouncing gay rights is an argument in and of itself, but shooting down gay rights when you yourself is gay just doesn't hold water. It should also be noted that many of the above men are also married, and cheating is pretty looked down upon in this country when it is convenient for Republicans to do so. Just ask Bill Clinton.

31. Republicans vs. The State

As you can see by now, Republicans have declared war on all different aspects of current America and American society. They pass bills on things they don't like, stop agendas they don't want, and shut down measures that don't fall in line with their political agenda. One of these aspects they have declared war on (at least when it suits them) is The State. As we have covered, Republicans like to tout that they are against Big Government, that they want the states to have more power, and the government to have less interference. This is the curtain they use to veil their arguments behind things like gun regulations. Still, just like with so many other weak arguments, these speculations all fall into one category. That category is, these demands only apply to things that Republicans don't like, but should be ignored on things that they do.

In 2014, the District of Columbia finally settled a long standing issue in this country. They decriminalized marijuana. This was huge news for the many who had been seeking such a bill for years. Under the new rules, it made it so that being caught with weed would not be as severe as it had been in the past. Getting caught with the substance, under the new law, makes it so you would only get a $25 ticket. A much better deal than going to jail, which is what would have happened under past regulations. This move to lower the penalty for possession to a $25 ticket was openly opposed by many member of the Republican Party, but that doesn't make much sense based on their own feelings about state regulations. In fact, based on their own testimonies, and the values that have been covered in this guide, the Republicans should be very exciting at this move.

The act of decriminalizing marijuana is a perfect example of a state making its own regulations and passing its own laws. You know, what Republicans have been saying they wanted for years. However, as the subject here is marijuana possession, Republicans are in fact not happy at all. They are quite angry. Is this because they have any problems with the process? Of course not. It has to do with the subject matter. When things such as gay marriage or abortion pop up or differentiate in states, Republicans are on the front lines. They claim that state rights are much more important than national rights. But this is only because such laws allow states to step around things they don't want coming to fruition. Marijuana possession has long been something Republicans have spoken against, and, as such, they do not like it when the states take the matter into their own hands. You just can't have it both ways.

On a whole range of issues, congressional Republicans would love to turn a city made up of mostly Democrats into a right-wing town. However, this is not the reality of the situation. They repeatedly make statements that they think judges and other authority figures should use the Constitution as guidelines. In this way, it is a document to be interpreted more than strictly followed. However, they also turn around and demand that judges step in to overrule laws they don't like. This kind of hypocrisy runs all throughout Republican arguments, but are rarer in the liberal agenda. This is mainly because liberals do not have such strict reasons for supporting hands-off policy, but rather they try to see the whole argument before making decisions on whether the state or national government should have power. Opinionated thinking does not always lead to flawed practices, but it does if you make up your mind before the argument even begins.

As it currently stands, the fate of the decriminalization law is still uncertain. Maryland Representative Andy Harris attached an amendment to the latest appropriations bill, which forbids D.C. from enforcing its new law. This bill passed the committee, but has yet to be voted on by the full House. As of now, the Obama Administration has threatened a new version of the appropriations bill, stating their opposition to multiple provisions in the bill's current version.

Republicans have made it clear that they want to re-criminalize marijuana, most likely because the reform is happening in their own backyard. The hypocrisy lies in the fact that conservative frequently want states to oppose the national government, but if a state does something they don't like, they want the national government to step in and change it. The system doesn't work quite like this, and it doesn't work in the way Republicans want it to. Still, that has never stopped them from trying to bend the rules before.

32. Draft Dodgers

While earlier in this guide we explored in detail just how little Republicans do not support our veterans when they come back from war, they do readily support our soldiers. They do this without worrying about the actual costs of war, or the lives lost. All that matters to them is that there are soldiers to fight the war, not what happens to those soldiers once the fighting begins. This passion for war makes perfect sense in line with classic Republican ideals. However, what does not make sense is how so many Republicans who have supported the war managed to dodge the draft themselves.

Many prominent Republicans have managed to avoid the draft throughout the years. This is a good starting point to understand the hypocrisy here, because it doesn't make sense that so many people who support soldiers and the war effort would be so resilient to keep themselves out of it. However, it is easier to send someone you don't know overseas than actually doing it yourself. The list of Republicans who have been found to dodge the draft goes on and on. Among the Republicans who avoided the war are Karl Rove, Tom Delay and Newt Gringrich. Former Senator Fred Thompson, former Speaker of the House Dennis Hastert and former House Majority Whip Roy Blunt all did not serve or avoided the draft.

To contrast, plenty of Democrats, even if they are not open to war, have spent their own time in the army. Rick Noriega, Democratic candidate for U.S. Senate from Texas, joined the U.S. Army in 1979; currently Lt. Colonel in Texas Army National Guard, served in Afghanistan. Senator Jim Webb (D-VA) was a part of the rifle platoon and company commander with the Fifth Marine Regiment in the An

Hoa Basin west of Danang. He was awarded the Navy Cross, the Silver Star Medal, two Bronze Star Medals, and two Purple Hearts. Representative Patrick Murphy, a Democrat from Pennsylvania had an extensive career in the U.S. Army from 1993-2004; earned Bronze Star and Presidential Unit Citation. Representative Phil Hare from Illinois served in the United States Army Reserve for six years. These are just a few examples, but show the difference between those who say they support the war but don't, and those who do not support the war but still understand the importance of fighting for this nation.

While the above examples show good examples of Republicans not following through on the things they say, there is no better example of draft dodging that ex-Republican candidate Mitt Romney. This goes back during the days of the Vietnam War. At that time, Romney participated in pro-draft registrations to support sending young Americans to fight in Vietnam, which turned out to be one of the most violent and controversial wars in history. Yet, when it came time for Romney to fight in the war himself, he was nowhere to be found. Romney, instead of entering the war effort, successfully managed to dodge the draft.

It isn't easy to dodge the draft, but you can if you serve the Mormon Church. Serving the Church allowed Romney to successfully stay out of Vietnam, and gave him a way to stay away from the war effort. During his campaign in 2012, the war came back to Romney when he was asked about sending his own sons overseas. He has five, but no intention of putting any of them into the war effort, that's for other people's children. Most likely, the war becomes all too real for ones removed such as Romney when their own kin is involved, but he claimed the reasons his sons are staying home was because they had a service to the church. He also made the somewhat see-

126

through argument that his sons were actually serving their country through helping his campaign.

Really? Is helping a millionaire try to become president serving the nation in the same way that someone alone in Kuwait, thousands of miles away from their family and friends, risking their life for the freedom we have, is? It doesn't seem so on paper. It is all fine and well to support other people you don't know going to war, but things change when it is your own flesh and blood. Romney already gave his real insight into how he felt about war when he stayed as far away as he could. Keeping his sons away falls right in line with this type of action. In fact, it would be very interesting to see how the ex-candidate and his family would feel about the war if they actually had to send their own. Probably, based on how we have witnessed Republicans handle so many situations, they would change their mind pretty darn fast.

33. I Love America?

While we have looked at a vast number of different topics and talking points that have stretched all through this guide, we end on a the topic that all of this is really about: America. Barack Obama has gotten a lot of flack from the Republican Party and its members over the course of his two terms. They have criticized his foreign and domestic policies, challenged his reforms and outright tried to stop a lot the progress he has hoped to achieve. However, despite all of this, they are still, under it all, Americans. While there may be differences between Republicans and Democrats, between the right and left wing, every person in both parties (even if they were born in Canada or Hawaii) calls this great country home. Here, in the last stage of hypocrisy we will look at, we will see if Republicans, in all of their glory, truly do love America.

The man at the center of this topic if Former New York City Mayor Rudy Giuliani. On February 20, 2015, Giuliani spoke at a private dinner party for Scott Walker, a likely 2016 candidate. "I do not believe, and I know this is a horrible thing to say, but I do not believe that the president loves America," the former mayor said "He doesn't love you. And he doesn't love me. He wasn't brought up the way you were brought up and I was brought up through love of this country." A very shocking thing to say, and a very surprising remark as well. Of course the president loves this country, it would be absurd to think anything else.

Democratic National Committee chair Debbie Wasserman Schultz weighed in, stating that "I rarely agreed with President Bush, but I never questioned his love for our country. I don't often agree with my Republican colleagues on the Hill, but I know they love America".

Very well said. This ties into the statement that everyone, especially the President, loves this country. Giuliani's statements were largely condemned, and of course he quickly retracted them when this happened. When asked about the remark, Giuliani said that he meant to say that, while Obama was still a patriot, he just did not like America in the same way past presidents had. While that is also not true, that is one of the best examples of the hypocrisy covered throughout these pages. To say that you love America but the president doesn't is absurd. This implies that Republicans love America, but Democrats don't.

After everything we have covered, and every part that we have seen, it should be rather obvious which party truly loves America. Republicans have repeatedly tried to deny many rights to American citizens. They have attacked progress, said contradictory statements and always put themselves before others. They have made it clear the masses do not matter to them, same with Latinos and women. They love the American ideal of freedom, but they do not think gays should have the freedom to marry. They love the idea of free speech and the right to protest, except if you are saying something they do not agree with. They also love the 2nd amendment to the point where they refuse to listen to any legislation to limit who has access to guns, even when mass shootings are still a common occurrence all across the nation. They want it to go both ways, but that is not the reality.

The biggest problem with the party is they only want things to go their way and no one else's. Just as with Paul Robertson, just as with big vs. small government, the Republican Party only wants things to happen when they need them to. Not everyone is going to agree, that is the nature of politics, but before they start calling out Obama for not loving the country, they should first look into their own party.

There are injustices happening all over this nation, and they are to blame for so many. If Republicans truly love America as they claim, it is high time that they start to show it.

www.ingramcontent.com/pod-product-compliance
Lightning Source LLC
Chambersburg PA
CBHW050351280326
41933CB00010BA/1420